Name _____

Minutes

1	2	3	4	5	6

Score

A
$$\begin{array}{r}4\\ \times 3\\ \hline\end{array}\quad\begin{array}{r}3\\ \times 1\\ \hline\end{array}\quad\begin{array}{r}2\\ \times 2\\ \hline\end{array}\quad\begin{array}{r}5\\ \times 5\\ \hline\end{array}\quad\begin{array}{r}3\\ \times 5\\ \hline\end{array}\quad\begin{array}{r}0\\ \times 3\\ \hline\end{array}\quad\begin{array}{r}4\\ \times 2\\ \hline\end{array}\quad\begin{array}{r}1\\ \times 4\\ \hline\end{array}\quad\begin{array}{r}2\\ \times 0\\ \hline\end{array}\quad\begin{array}{r}5\\ \times 2\\ \hline\end{array}$$

B
$$\begin{array}{r}5\\ \times 5\\ \hline\end{array}\quad\begin{array}{r}4\\ \times 2\\ \hline\end{array}\quad\begin{array}{r}0\\ \times 5\\ \hline\end{array}\quad\begin{array}{r}4\\ \times 4\\ \hline\end{array}\quad\begin{array}{r}1\\ \times 5\\ \hline\end{array}\quad\begin{array}{r}2\\ \times 3\\ \hline\end{array}\quad\begin{array}{r}5\\ \times 4\\ \hline\end{array}\quad\begin{array}{r}2\\ \times 5\\ \hline\end{array}\quad\begin{array}{r}0\\ \times 1\\ \hline\end{array}\quad\begin{array}{r}3\\ \times 3\\ \hline\end{array}$$

C
$$\begin{array}{r}0\\ \times 2\\ \hline\end{array}\quad\begin{array}{r}3\\ \times 1\\ \hline\end{array}\quad\begin{array}{r}5\\ \times 1\\ \hline\end{array}\quad\begin{array}{r}4\\ \times 5\\ \hline\end{array}\quad\begin{array}{r}3\\ \times 0\\ \hline\end{array}\quad\begin{array}{r}1\\ \times 1\\ \hline\end{array}\quad\begin{array}{r}2\\ \times 2\\ \hline\end{array}\quad\begin{array}{r}0\\ \times 1\\ \hline\end{array}\quad\begin{array}{r}4\\ \times 0\\ \hline\end{array}\quad\begin{array}{r}1\\ \times 2\\ \hline\end{array}$$

D
$$\begin{array}{r}2\\ \times 3\\ \hline\end{array}\quad\begin{array}{r}3\\ \times 4\\ \hline\end{array}\quad\begin{array}{r}2\\ \times 0\\ \hline\end{array}\quad\begin{array}{r}5\\ \times 3\\ \hline\end{array}\quad\begin{array}{r}2\\ \times 5\\ \hline\end{array}\quad\begin{array}{r}4\\ \times 4\\ \hline\end{array}\quad\begin{array}{r}0\\ \times 0\\ \hline\end{array}\quad\begin{array}{r}3\\ \times 1\\ \hline\end{array}\quad\begin{array}{r}5\\ \times 2\\ \hline\end{array}\quad\begin{array}{r}1\\ \times 2\\ \hline\end{array}$$

E
$$\begin{array}{r}5\\ \times 0\\ \hline\end{array}\quad\begin{array}{r}1\\ \times 3\\ \hline\end{array}\quad\begin{array}{r}2\\ \times 1\\ \hline\end{array}\quad\begin{array}{r}3\\ \times 2\\ \hline\end{array}\quad\begin{array}{r}0\\ \times 2\\ \hline\end{array}\quad\begin{array}{r}4\\ \times 1\\ \hline\end{array}\quad\begin{array}{r}3\\ \times 4\\ \hline\end{array}\quad\begin{array}{r}1\\ \times 0\\ \hline\end{array}\quad\begin{array}{r}3\\ \times 5\\ \hline\end{array}\quad\begin{array}{r}5\\ \times 1\\ \hline\end{array}$$

F
$$\begin{array}{r}2\\ \times 4\\ \hline\end{array}\quad\begin{array}{r}0\\ \times 5\\ \hline\end{array}\quad\begin{array}{r}0\\ \times 0\\ \hline\end{array}\quad\begin{array}{r}4\\ \times 2\\ \hline\end{array}\quad\begin{array}{r}3\\ \times 3\\ \hline\end{array}\quad\begin{array}{r}1\\ \times 5\\ \hline\end{array}\quad\begin{array}{r}1\\ \times 1\\ \hline\end{array}\quad\begin{array}{r}4\\ \times 1\\ \hline\end{array}\quad\begin{array}{r}3\\ \times 0\\ \hline\end{array}\quad\begin{array}{r}0\\ \times 4\\ \hline\end{array}$$

G
$$\begin{array}{r}5\\ \times 4\\ \hline\end{array}\quad\begin{array}{r}2\\ \times 1\\ \hline\end{array}\quad\begin{array}{r}0\\ \times 0\\ \hline\end{array}\quad\begin{array}{r}1\\ \times 5\\ \hline\end{array}\quad\begin{array}{r}5\\ \times 0\\ \hline\end{array}\quad\begin{array}{r}4\\ \times 4\\ \hline\end{array}\quad\begin{array}{r}1\\ \times 2\\ \hline\end{array}\quad\begin{array}{r}2\\ \times 5\\ \hline\end{array}\quad\begin{array}{r}5\\ \times 1\\ \hline\end{array}\quad\begin{array}{r}2\\ \times 4\\ \hline\end{array}$$

H
$$\begin{array}{r}4\\ \times 0\\ \hline\end{array}\quad\begin{array}{r}5\\ \times 2\\ \hline\end{array}\quad\begin{array}{r}1\\ \times 4\\ \hline\end{array}\quad\begin{array}{r}3\\ \times 0\\ \hline\end{array}\quad\begin{array}{r}3\\ \times 2\\ \hline\end{array}\quad\begin{array}{r}1\\ \times 3\\ \hline\end{array}\quad\begin{array}{r}5\\ \times 3\\ \hline\end{array}\quad\begin{array}{r}0\\ \times 1\\ \hline\end{array}\quad\begin{array}{r}2\\ \times 2\\ \hline\end{array}\quad\begin{array}{r}4\\ \times 3\\ \hline\end{array}$$

I
$$\begin{array}{r}4\\ \times 5\\ \hline\end{array}\quad\begin{array}{r}0\\ \times 3\\ \hline\end{array}\quad\begin{array}{r}3\\ \times 2\\ \hline\end{array}\quad\begin{array}{r}4\\ \times 3\\ \hline\end{array}\quad\begin{array}{r}1\\ \times 1\\ \hline\end{array}\quad\begin{array}{r}2\\ \times 3\\ \hline\end{array}\quad\begin{array}{r}3\\ \times 5\\ \hline\end{array}\quad\begin{array}{r}2\\ \times 1\\ \hline\end{array}\quad\begin{array}{r}1\\ \times 4\\ \hline\end{array}\quad\begin{array}{r}5\\ \times 5\\ \hline\end{array}$$

J
$$\begin{array}{r}3\\ \times 4\\ \hline\end{array}\quad\begin{array}{r}1\\ \times 0\\ \hline\end{array}\quad\begin{array}{r}5\\ \times 4\\ \hline\end{array}\quad\begin{array}{r}4\\ \times 1\\ \hline\end{array}\quad\begin{array}{r}5\\ \times 3\\ \hline\end{array}\quad\begin{array}{r}0\\ \times 4\\ \hline\end{array}\quad\begin{array}{r}4\\ \times 5\\ \hline\end{array}\quad\begin{array}{r}1\\ \times 3\\ \hline\end{array}\quad\begin{array}{r}2\\ \times 4\\ \hline\end{array}\quad\begin{array}{r}3\\ \times 3\\ \hline\end{array}$$

Name _____

Minutes

| 1 | 2 | 3 | 4 | 5 | 6 |

Score

	A									
A	1 ×3	2 ×5	1 ×4	4 ×3	4 ×5	0 ×1	3 ×3	4 ×0	2 ×3	3 ×4
B	0 ×5	5 ×5	4 ×1	2 ×4	1 ×1	5 ×2	4 ×4	2 ×1	3 ×0	5 ×3
C	5 ×1	0 ×3	3 ×4	2 ×3	1 ×5	4 ×0	3 ×2	5 ×2	1 ×3	1 ×2
D	2 ×0	3 ×3	5 ×1	0 ×5	3 ×1	4 ×5	4 ×2	0 ×0	1 ×1	5 ×5
E	4 ×4	2 ×2	1 ×0	4 ×1	4 ×3	0 ×2	3 ×5	2 ×1	5 ×0	5 ×3
F	1 ×5	3 ×3	0 ×1	2 ×5	1 ×4	2 ×2	4 ×5	0 ×4	3 ×0	3 ×5
G	2 ×4	1 ×2	4 ×1	1 ×1	5 ×2	2 ×3	3 ×1	4 ×3	3 ×2	0 ×3
H	2 ×1	3 ×0	5 ×1	1 ×3	3 ×5	4 ×0	5 ×4	0 ×2	5 ×5	0 ×1
I	0 ×4	4 ×2	5 ×3	2 ×2	2 ×4	1 ×0	3 ×4	5 ×4	2 ×0	1 ×4
J	4 ×2	0 ×0	5 ×0	3 ×2	1 ×5	3 ×1	5 ×4	2 ×5	1 ×2	4 ×4

2

© Carson-Dellosa Publ. CD-0926

Name _____

Minutes

1	2	3	4	5	6

Score

A	6 ×2	0 ×5	7 ×5	5 ×6	3 ×3	7 ×3	1 ×5	4 ×4	4 ×6	5 ×4
B	3 ×0	7 ×7	2 ×3	1 ×1	3 ×6	2 ×5	6 ×5	4 ×1	0 ×2	7 ×5
C	6 ×5	3 ×6	4 ×3	7 ×1	1 ×0	4 ×7	5 ×3	2 ×2	7 ×6	3 ×5
D	5 ×7	1 ×4	5 ×0	3 ×2	4 ×3	0 ×0	6 ×1	4 ×5	2 ×7	6 ×2
E	2 ×1	5 ×3	7 ×4	0 ×4	4 ×2	6 ×6	4 ×5	3 ×2	2 ×5	7 ×0
F	7 ×2	3 ×5	2 ×4	5 ×5	1 ×6	3 ×4	5 ×2	0 ×7	3 ×7	6 ×4
G	5 ×4	4 ×2	0 ×1	6 ×7	6 ×3	2 ×6	2 ×7	7 ×7	1 ×3	2 ×2
H	1 ×2	7 ×3	6 ×6	4 ×4	5 ×2	2 ×0	5 ×7	4 ×6	3 ×1	6 ×7
I	6 ×0	3 ×4	1 ×7	7 ×4	6 ×3	5 ×1	0 ×3	6 ×4	2 ×4	3 ×3
J	4 ×0	2 ×3	7 ×6	2 ×6	0 ×6	4 ×7	5 ×5	3 ×7	5 ×6	7 ×2

Name _____

Minutes
1	2	3	4	5	6

Score

A $\begin{array}{r}6\\ \times 6\\ \hline\end{array}$ $\begin{array}{r}1\\ \times 3\\ \hline\end{array}$ $\begin{array}{r}7\\ \times 0\\ \hline\end{array}$ $\begin{array}{r}4\\ \times 2\\ \hline\end{array}$ $\begin{array}{r}0\\ \times 5\\ \hline\end{array}$ $\begin{array}{r}4\\ \times 4\\ \hline\end{array}$ $\begin{array}{r}5\\ \times 6\\ \hline\end{array}$ $\begin{array}{r}3\\ \times 2\\ \hline\end{array}$ $\begin{array}{r}3\\ \times 6\\ \hline\end{array}$ $\begin{array}{r}5\\ \times 4\\ \hline\end{array}$

B $\begin{array}{r}6\\ \times 5\\ \hline\end{array}$ $\begin{array}{r}5\\ \times 1\\ \hline\end{array}$ $\begin{array}{r}1\\ \times 7\\ \hline\end{array}$ $\begin{array}{r}3\\ \times 7\\ \hline\end{array}$ $\begin{array}{r}7\\ \times 4\\ \hline\end{array}$ $\begin{array}{r}3\\ \times 2\\ \hline\end{array}$ $\begin{array}{r}4\\ \times 6\\ \hline\end{array}$ $\begin{array}{r}0\\ \times 2\\ \hline\end{array}$ $\begin{array}{r}6\\ \times 1\\ \hline\end{array}$ $\begin{array}{r}2\\ \times 6\\ \hline\end{array}$

C $\begin{array}{r}4\\ \times 5\\ \hline\end{array}$ $\begin{array}{r}3\\ \times 3\\ \hline\end{array}$ $\begin{array}{r}7\\ \times 7\\ \hline\end{array}$ $\begin{array}{r}2\\ \times 4\\ \hline\end{array}$ $\begin{array}{r}5\\ \times 6\\ \hline\end{array}$ $\begin{array}{r}1\\ \times 0\\ \hline\end{array}$ $\begin{array}{r}7\\ \times 2\\ \hline\end{array}$ $\begin{array}{r}6\\ \times 3\\ \hline\end{array}$ $\begin{array}{r}4\\ \times 7\\ \hline\end{array}$ $\begin{array}{r}7\\ \times 6\\ \hline\end{array}$

D $\begin{array}{r}5\\ \times 5\\ \hline\end{array}$ $\begin{array}{r}0\\ \times 0\\ \hline\end{array}$ $\begin{array}{r}3\\ \times 1\\ \hline\end{array}$ $\begin{array}{r}6\\ \times 7\\ \hline\end{array}$ $\begin{array}{r}3\\ \times 5\\ \hline\end{array}$ $\begin{array}{r}6\\ \times 4\\ \hline\end{array}$ $\begin{array}{r}7\\ \times 5\\ \hline\end{array}$ $\begin{array}{r}1\\ \times 2\\ \hline\end{array}$ $\begin{array}{r}4\\ \times 0\\ \hline\end{array}$ $\begin{array}{r}5\\ \times 7\\ \hline\end{array}$

E $\begin{array}{r}7\\ \times 3\\ \hline\end{array}$ $\begin{array}{r}2\\ \times 0\\ \hline\end{array}$ $\begin{array}{r}6\\ \times 2\\ \hline\end{array}$ $\begin{array}{r}4\\ \times 5\\ \hline\end{array}$ $\begin{array}{r}3\\ \times 1\\ \hline\end{array}$ $\begin{array}{r}0\\ \times 4\\ \hline\end{array}$ $\begin{array}{r}4\\ \times 7\\ \hline\end{array}$ $\begin{array}{r}5\\ \times 2\\ \hline\end{array}$ $\begin{array}{r}7\\ \times 1\\ \hline\end{array}$ $\begin{array}{r}4\\ \times 3\\ \hline\end{array}$

F $\begin{array}{r}1\\ \times 5\\ \hline\end{array}$ $\begin{array}{r}5\\ \times 3\\ \hline\end{array}$ $\begin{array}{r}6\\ \times 0\\ \hline\end{array}$ $\begin{array}{r}3\\ \times 7\\ \hline\end{array}$ $\begin{array}{r}4\\ \times 3\\ \hline\end{array}$ $\begin{array}{r}5\\ \times 7\\ \hline\end{array}$ $\begin{array}{r}4\\ \times 1\\ \hline\end{array}$ $\begin{array}{r}3\\ \times 4\\ \hline\end{array}$ $\begin{array}{r}0\\ \times 7\\ \hline\end{array}$ $\begin{array}{r}4\\ \times 2\\ \hline\end{array}$

G $\begin{array}{r}7\\ \times 7\\ \hline\end{array}$ $\begin{array}{r}2\\ \times 5\\ \hline\end{array}$ $\begin{array}{r}6\\ \times 4\\ \hline\end{array}$ $\begin{array}{r}0\\ \times 1\\ \hline\end{array}$ $\begin{array}{r}5\\ \times 4\\ \hline\end{array}$ $\begin{array}{r}2\\ \times 1\\ \hline\end{array}$ $\begin{array}{r}3\\ \times 4\\ \hline\end{array}$ $\begin{array}{r}6\\ \times 7\\ \hline\end{array}$ $\begin{array}{r}4\\ \times 1\\ \hline\end{array}$ $\begin{array}{r}1\\ \times 6\\ \hline\end{array}$

H $\begin{array}{r}4\\ \times 4\\ \hline\end{array}$ $\begin{array}{r}6\\ \times 2\\ \hline\end{array}$ $\begin{array}{r}2\\ \times 3\\ \hline\end{array}$ $\begin{array}{r}5\\ \times 0\\ \hline\end{array}$ $\begin{array}{r}1\\ \times 1\\ \hline\end{array}$ $\begin{array}{r}7\\ \times 6\\ \hline\end{array}$ $\begin{array}{r}5\\ \times 2\\ \hline\end{array}$ $\begin{array}{r}3\\ \times 0\\ \hline\end{array}$ $\begin{array}{r}3\\ \times 6\\ \hline\end{array}$ $\begin{array}{r}7\\ \times 3\\ \hline\end{array}$

I $\begin{array}{r}2\\ \times 1\\ \hline\end{array}$ $\begin{array}{r}3\\ \times 3\\ \hline\end{array}$ $\begin{array}{r}6\\ \times 1\\ \hline\end{array}$ $\begin{array}{r}1\\ \times 4\\ \hline\end{array}$ $\begin{array}{r}6\\ \times 6\\ \hline\end{array}$ $\begin{array}{r}7\\ \times 1\\ \hline\end{array}$ $\begin{array}{r}0\\ \times 3\\ \hline\end{array}$ $\begin{array}{r}7\\ \times 4\\ \hline\end{array}$ $\begin{array}{r}2\\ \times 7\\ \hline\end{array}$ $\begin{array}{r}6\\ \times 5\\ \hline\end{array}$

J $\begin{array}{r}7\\ \times 5\\ \hline\end{array}$ $\begin{array}{r}0\\ \times 6\\ \hline\end{array}$ $\begin{array}{r}5\\ \times 1\\ \hline\end{array}$ $\begin{array}{r}5\\ \times 3\\ \hline\end{array}$ $\begin{array}{r}7\\ \times 2\\ \hline\end{array}$ $\begin{array}{r}2\\ \times 2\\ \hline\end{array}$ $\begin{array}{r}6\\ \times 3\\ \hline\end{array}$ $\begin{array}{r}4\\ \times 6\\ \hline\end{array}$ $\begin{array}{r}5\\ \times 5\\ \hline\end{array}$ $\begin{array}{r}3\\ \times 5\\ \hline\end{array}$

Name _____

Minutes						Score
1	2	3	4	5	6	

A
$\begin{array}{r}8\\ \times 0\\ \hline\end{array}$
$\begin{array}{r}5\\ \times 2\\ \hline\end{array}$
$\begin{array}{r}0\\ \times 4\\ \hline\end{array}$
$\begin{array}{r}9\\ \times 2\\ \hline\end{array}$
$\begin{array}{r}4\\ \times 5\\ \hline\end{array}$
$\begin{array}{r}2\\ \times 7\\ \hline\end{array}$
$\begin{array}{r}7\\ \times 6\\ \hline\end{array}$
$\begin{array}{r}3\\ \times 6\\ \hline\end{array}$
$\begin{array}{r}6\\ \times 7\\ \hline\end{array}$
$\begin{array}{r}1\\ \times 1\\ \hline\end{array}$

B
$\begin{array}{r}5\\ \times 8\\ \hline\end{array}$
$\begin{array}{r}2\\ \times 3\\ \hline\end{array}$
$\begin{array}{r}6\\ \times 4\\ \hline\end{array}$
$\begin{array}{r}4\\ \times 2\\ \hline\end{array}$
$\begin{array}{r}9\\ \times 7\\ \hline\end{array}$
$\begin{array}{r}0\\ \times 9\\ \hline\end{array}$
$\begin{array}{r}3\\ \times 1\\ \hline\end{array}$
$\begin{array}{r}7\\ \times 3\\ \hline\end{array}$
$\begin{array}{r}1\\ \times 6\\ \hline\end{array}$
$\begin{array}{r}8\\ \times 4\\ \hline\end{array}$

C
$\begin{array}{r}7\\ \times 5\\ \hline\end{array}$
$\begin{array}{r}9\\ \times 1\\ \hline\end{array}$
$\begin{array}{r}1\\ \times 4\\ \hline\end{array}$
$\begin{array}{r}6\\ \times 1\\ \hline\end{array}$
$\begin{array}{r}2\\ \times 0\\ \hline\end{array}$
$\begin{array}{r}5\\ \times 3\\ \hline\end{array}$
$\begin{array}{r}9\\ \times 9\\ \hline\end{array}$
$\begin{array}{r}4\\ \times 3\\ \hline\end{array}$
$\begin{array}{r}9\\ \times 5\\ \hline\end{array}$
$\begin{array}{r}0\\ \times 3\\ \hline\end{array}$

D
$\begin{array}{r}2\\ \times 8\\ \hline\end{array}$
$\begin{array}{r}6\\ \times 6\\ \hline\end{array}$
$\begin{array}{r}4\\ \times 7\\ \hline\end{array}$
$\begin{array}{r}0\\ \times 1\\ \hline\end{array}$
$\begin{array}{r}7\\ \times 9\\ \hline\end{array}$
$\begin{array}{r}3\\ \times 3\\ \hline\end{array}$
$\begin{array}{r}5\\ \times 5\\ \hline\end{array}$
$\begin{array}{r}1\\ \times 2\\ \hline\end{array}$
$\begin{array}{r}4\\ \times 0\\ \hline\end{array}$
$\begin{array}{r}8\\ \times 1\\ \hline\end{array}$

E
$\begin{array}{r}0\\ \times 6\\ \hline\end{array}$
$\begin{array}{r}8\\ \times 8\\ \hline\end{array}$
$\begin{array}{r}3\\ \times 5\\ \hline\end{array}$
$\begin{array}{r}8\\ \times 3\\ \hline\end{array}$
$\begin{array}{r}2\\ \times 2\\ \hline\end{array}$
$\begin{array}{r}5\\ \times 1\\ \hline\end{array}$
$\begin{array}{r}1\\ \times 7\\ \hline\end{array}$
$\begin{array}{r}4\\ \times 8\\ \hline\end{array}$
$\begin{array}{r}7\\ \times 0\\ \hline\end{array}$
$\begin{array}{r}3\\ \times 9\\ \hline\end{array}$

F
$\begin{array}{r}7\\ \times 1\\ \hline\end{array}$
$\begin{array}{r}2\\ \times 6\\ \hline\end{array}$
$\begin{array}{r}8\\ \times 5\\ \hline\end{array}$
$\begin{array}{r}1\\ \times 3\\ \hline\end{array}$
$\begin{array}{r}6\\ \times 0\\ \hline\end{array}$
$\begin{array}{r}3\\ \times 2\\ \hline\end{array}$
$\begin{array}{r}5\\ \times 7\\ \hline\end{array}$
$\begin{array}{r}0\\ \times 8\\ \hline\end{array}$
$\begin{array}{r}6\\ \times 3\\ \hline\end{array}$
$\begin{array}{r}2\\ \times 4\\ \hline\end{array}$

G
$\begin{array}{r}2\\ \times 9\\ \hline\end{array}$
$\begin{array}{r}9\\ \times 0\\ \hline\end{array}$
$\begin{array}{r}0\\ \times 2\\ \hline\end{array}$
$\begin{array}{r}5\\ \times 4\\ \hline\end{array}$
$\begin{array}{r}4\\ \times 4\\ \hline\end{array}$
$\begin{array}{r}7\\ \times 8\\ \hline\end{array}$
$\begin{array}{r}1\\ \times 0\\ \hline\end{array}$
$\begin{array}{r}6\\ \times 9\\ \hline\end{array}$
$\begin{array}{r}3\\ \times 0\\ \hline\end{array}$
$\begin{array}{r}9\\ \times 4\\ \hline\end{array}$

H
$\begin{array}{r}8\\ \times 9\\ \hline\end{array}$
$\begin{array}{r}2\\ \times 1\\ \hline\end{array}$
$\begin{array}{r}5\\ \times 9\\ \hline\end{array}$
$\begin{array}{r}7\\ \times 4\\ \hline\end{array}$
$\begin{array}{r}0\\ \times 5\\ \hline\end{array}$
$\begin{array}{r}4\\ \times 1\\ \hline\end{array}$
$\begin{array}{r}3\\ \times 7\\ \hline\end{array}$
$\begin{array}{r}9\\ \times 8\\ \hline\end{array}$
$\begin{array}{r}1\\ \times 9\\ \hline\end{array}$
$\begin{array}{r}8\\ \times 7\\ \hline\end{array}$

I
$\begin{array}{r}4\\ \times 6\\ \hline\end{array}$
$\begin{array}{r}9\\ \times 6\\ \hline\end{array}$
$\begin{array}{r}1\\ \times 8\\ \hline\end{array}$
$\begin{array}{r}6\\ \times 5\\ \hline\end{array}$
$\begin{array}{r}3\\ \times 4\\ \hline\end{array}$
$\begin{array}{r}5\\ \times 0\\ \hline\end{array}$
$\begin{array}{r}2\\ \times 5\\ \hline\end{array}$
$\begin{array}{r}8\\ \times 2\\ \hline\end{array}$
$\begin{array}{r}0\\ \times 0\\ \hline\end{array}$
$\begin{array}{r}7\\ \times 7\\ \hline\end{array}$

J
$\begin{array}{r}1\\ \times 5\\ \hline\end{array}$
$\begin{array}{r}9\\ \times 3\\ \hline\end{array}$
$\begin{array}{r}6\\ \times 2\\ \hline\end{array}$
$\begin{array}{r}0\\ \times 7\\ \hline\end{array}$
$\begin{array}{r}8\\ \times 6\\ \hline\end{array}$
$\begin{array}{r}5\\ \times 6\\ \hline\end{array}$
$\begin{array}{r}4\\ \times 9\\ \hline\end{array}$
$\begin{array}{r}3\\ \times 8\\ \hline\end{array}$
$\begin{array}{r}7\\ \times 2\\ \hline\end{array}$
$\begin{array}{r}6\\ \times 8\\ \hline\end{array}$

Name _____

Minutes						Score
1	2	3	4	5	6	

A	8 ×2	4 ×8	1 ×3	6 ×7	3 ×0	9 ×3	2 ×4	5 ×6	0 ×4	7 ×5
B	7 ×2	2 ×9	6 ×0	9 ×6	0 ×2	3 ×7	5 ×9	4 ×6	8 ×5	1 ×5
C	4 ×1	8 ×8	0 ×7	6 ×4	5 ×2	9 ×4	1 ×0	7 ×8	2 ×8	3 ×3
D	5 ×3	6 ×8	2 ×3	8 ×4	4 ×3	1 ×8	7 ×4	0 ×0	3 ×6	9 ×1
E	3 ×4	1 ×6	9 ×0	5 ×7	0 ×5	8 ×9	6 ×6	7 ×1	2 ×0	4 ×5
F	0 ×9	9 ×8	3 ×1	7 ×7	2 ×5	6 ×1	4 ×0	1 ×2	8 ×7	5 ×5
G	6 ×5	3 ×9	0 ×1	9 ×7	4 ×2	5 ×1	1 ×1	8 ×1	2 ×2	7 ×9
H	5 ×8	1 ×4	7 ×3	3 ×5	9 ×5	2 ×7	4 ×9	6 ×2	8 ×3	0 ×8
I	2 ×1	8 ×6	7 ×0	1 ×9	9 ×9	4 ×4	0 ×3	7 ×6	3 ×2	5 ×4
J	4 ×7	0 ×6	6 ×9	3 ×8	5 ×0	2 ×6	8 ×0	9 ×2	1 ×7	6 ×3

Name _____

Minutes

1	2	3	4	5	6

Score

A
$\begin{array}{r}9\\\times7\\\hline\end{array}$
$\begin{array}{r}4\\\times8\\\hline\end{array}$
$\begin{array}{r}3\\\times9\\\hline\end{array}$
$\begin{array}{r}6\\\times5\\\hline\end{array}$
$\begin{array}{r}1\\\times0\\\hline\end{array}$
$\begin{array}{r}6\\\times2\\\hline\end{array}$
$\begin{array}{r}2\\\times3\\\hline\end{array}$
$\begin{array}{r}8\\\times2\\\hline\end{array}$
$\begin{array}{r}1\\\times6\\\hline\end{array}$
$\begin{array}{r}7\\\times0\\\hline\end{array}$

B
$\begin{array}{r}2\\\times6\\\hline\end{array}$
$\begin{array}{r}5\\\times5\\\hline\end{array}$
$\begin{array}{r}0\\\times3\\\hline\end{array}$
$\begin{array}{r}8\\\times7\\\hline\end{array}$
$\begin{array}{r}3\\\times3\\\hline\end{array}$
$\begin{array}{r}4\\\times0\\\hline\end{array}$
$\begin{array}{r}9\\\times9\\\hline\end{array}$
$\begin{array}{r}0\\\times8\\\hline\end{array}$
$\begin{array}{r}6\\\times9\\\hline\end{array}$
$\begin{array}{r}7\\\times6\\\hline\end{array}$

C
$\begin{array}{r}7\\\times9\\\hline\end{array}$
$\begin{array}{r}4\\\times3\\\hline\end{array}$
$\begin{array}{r}7\\\times3\\\hline\end{array}$
$\begin{array}{r}2\\\times0\\\hline\end{array}$
$\begin{array}{r}7\\\times5\\\hline\end{array}$
$\begin{array}{r}0\\\times0\\\hline\end{array}$
$\begin{array}{r}1\\\times3\\\hline\end{array}$
$\begin{array}{r}9\\\times5\\\hline\end{array}$
$\begin{array}{r}4\\\times5\\\hline\end{array}$
$\begin{array}{r}2\\\times7\\\hline\end{array}$

D
$\begin{array}{r}1\\\times7\\\hline\end{array}$
$\begin{array}{r}9\\\times3\\\hline\end{array}$
$\begin{array}{r}3\\\times2\\\hline\end{array}$
$\begin{array}{r}0\\\times9\\\hline\end{array}$
$\begin{array}{r}5\\\times8\\\hline\end{array}$
$\begin{array}{r}8\\\times0\\\hline\end{array}$
$\begin{array}{r}2\\\times2\\\hline\end{array}$
$\begin{array}{r}4\\\times9\\\hline\end{array}$
$\begin{array}{r}5\\\times0\\\hline\end{array}$
$\begin{array}{r}8\\\times6\\\hline\end{array}$

E
$\begin{array}{r}4\\\times7\\\hline\end{array}$
$\begin{array}{r}3\\\times8\\\hline\end{array}$
$\begin{array}{r}2\\\times9\\\hline\end{array}$
$\begin{array}{r}6\\\times1\\\hline\end{array}$
$\begin{array}{r}5\\\times2\\\hline\end{array}$
$\begin{array}{r}1\\\times2\\\hline\end{array}$
$\begin{array}{r}6\\\times8\\\hline\end{array}$
$\begin{array}{r}9\\\times1\\\hline\end{array}$
$\begin{array}{r}0\\\times4\\\hline\end{array}$
$\begin{array}{r}6\\\times3\\\hline\end{array}$

F
$\begin{array}{r}3\\\times5\\\hline\end{array}$
$\begin{array}{r}5\\\times4\\\hline\end{array}$
$\begin{array}{r}0\\\times6\\\hline\end{array}$
$\begin{array}{r}7\\\times8\\\hline\end{array}$
$\begin{array}{r}4\\\times2\\\hline\end{array}$
$\begin{array}{r}2\\\times8\\\hline\end{array}$
$\begin{array}{r}7\\\times1\\\hline\end{array}$
$\begin{array}{r}3\\\times4\\\hline\end{array}$
$\begin{array}{r}0\\\times7\\\hline\end{array}$
$\begin{array}{r}8\\\times1\\\hline\end{array}$

G
$\begin{array}{r}8\\\times5\\\hline\end{array}$
$\begin{array}{r}3\\\times1\\\hline\end{array}$
$\begin{array}{r}8\\\times3\\\hline\end{array}$
$\begin{array}{r}0\\\times1\\\hline\end{array}$
$\begin{array}{r}5\\\times7\\\hline\end{array}$
$\begin{array}{r}9\\\times8\\\hline\end{array}$
$\begin{array}{r}1\\\times5\\\hline\end{array}$
$\begin{array}{r}4\\\times4\\\hline\end{array}$
$\begin{array}{r}9\\\times4\\\hline\end{array}$
$\begin{array}{r}2\\\times5\\\hline\end{array}$

H
$\begin{array}{r}0\\\times5\\\hline\end{array}$
$\begin{array}{r}9\\\times6\\\hline\end{array}$
$\begin{array}{r}6\\\times0\\\hline\end{array}$
$\begin{array}{r}3\\\times7\\\hline\end{array}$
$\begin{array}{r}2\\\times1\\\hline\end{array}$
$\begin{array}{r}8\\\times8\\\hline\end{array}$
$\begin{array}{r}6\\\times4\\\hline\end{array}$
$\begin{array}{r}1\\\times8\\\hline\end{array}$
$\begin{array}{r}9\\\times0\\\hline\end{array}$
$\begin{array}{r}6\\\times6\\\hline\end{array}$

I
$\begin{array}{r}7\\\times7\\\hline\end{array}$
$\begin{array}{r}5\\\times9\\\hline\end{array}$
$\begin{array}{r}3\\\times0\\\hline\end{array}$
$\begin{array}{r}7\\\times2\\\hline\end{array}$
$\begin{array}{r}1\\\times1\\\hline\end{array}$
$\begin{array}{r}4\\\times1\\\hline\end{array}$
$\begin{array}{r}6\\\times7\\\hline\end{array}$
$\begin{array}{r}5\\\times3\\\hline\end{array}$
$\begin{array}{r}8\\\times9\\\hline\end{array}$
$\begin{array}{r}1\\\times9\\\hline\end{array}$

J
$\begin{array}{r}2\\\times4\\\hline\end{array}$
$\begin{array}{r}5\\\times6\\\hline\end{array}$
$\begin{array}{r}1\\\times4\\\hline\end{array}$
$\begin{array}{r}4\\\times6\\\hline\end{array}$
$\begin{array}{r}8\\\times4\\\hline\end{array}$
$\begin{array}{r}3\\\times6\\\hline\end{array}$
$\begin{array}{r}5\\\times1\\\hline\end{array}$
$\begin{array}{r}0\\\times2\\\hline\end{array}$
$\begin{array}{r}7\\\times4\\\hline\end{array}$
$\begin{array}{r}9\\\times2\\\hline\end{array}$

Name _____

Minutes

1	2	3	4	5	6

Score

A
$\begin{array}{r}8\\\times3\\\hline\end{array}$
$\begin{array}{r}9\\\times6\\\hline\end{array}$
$\begin{array}{r}4\\\times6\\\hline\end{array}$
$\begin{array}{r}9\\\times0\\\hline\end{array}$
$\begin{array}{r}1\\\times2\\\hline\end{array}$
$\begin{array}{r}3\\\times3\\\hline\end{array}$
$\begin{array}{r}0\\\times8\\\hline\end{array}$
$\begin{array}{r}9\\\times3\\\hline\end{array}$
$\begin{array}{r}5\\\times4\\\hline\end{array}$
$\begin{array}{r}2\\\times4\\\hline\end{array}$

B
$\begin{array}{r}1\\\times6\\\hline\end{array}$
$\begin{array}{r}7\\\times6\\\hline\end{array}$
$\begin{array}{r}0\\\times6\\\hline\end{array}$
$\begin{array}{r}5\\\times1\\\hline\end{array}$
$\begin{array}{r}4\\\times2\\\hline\end{array}$
$\begin{array}{r}3\\\times8\\\hline\end{array}$
$\begin{array}{r}7\\\times3\\\hline\end{array}$
$\begin{array}{r}0\\\times2\\\hline\end{array}$
$\begin{array}{r}6\\\times4\\\hline\end{array}$
$\begin{array}{r}5\\\times9\\\hline\end{array}$

C
$\begin{array}{r}8\\\times6\\\hline\end{array}$
$\begin{array}{r}2\\\times8\\\hline\end{array}$
$\begin{array}{r}8\\\times0\\\hline\end{array}$
$\begin{array}{r}1\\\times3\\\hline\end{array}$
$\begin{array}{r}6\\\times2\\\hline\end{array}$
$\begin{array}{r}5\\\times7\\\hline\end{array}$
$\begin{array}{r}2\\\times1\\\hline\end{array}$
$\begin{array}{r}6\\\times8\\\hline\end{array}$
$\begin{array}{r}3\\\times5\\\hline\end{array}$
$\begin{array}{r}8\\\times9\\\hline\end{array}$

D
$\begin{array}{r}7\\\times9\\\hline\end{array}$
$\begin{array}{r}1\\\times1\\\hline\end{array}$
$\begin{array}{r}0\\\times4\\\hline\end{array}$
$\begin{array}{r}7\\\times2\\\hline\end{array}$
$\begin{array}{r}4\\\times5\\\hline\end{array}$
$\begin{array}{r}3\\\times2\\\hline\end{array}$
$\begin{array}{r}5\\\times0\\\hline\end{array}$
$\begin{array}{r}9\\\times5\\\hline\end{array}$
$\begin{array}{r}0\\\times9\\\hline\end{array}$
$\begin{array}{r}8\\\times2\\\hline\end{array}$

E
$\begin{array}{r}4\\\times3\\\hline\end{array}$
$\begin{array}{r}1\\\times7\\\hline\end{array}$
$\begin{array}{r}9\\\times8\\\hline\end{array}$
$\begin{array}{r}6\\\times7\\\hline\end{array}$
$\begin{array}{r}0\\\times1\\\hline\end{array}$
$\begin{array}{r}2\\\times7\\\hline\end{array}$
$\begin{array}{r}7\\\times5\\\hline\end{array}$
$\begin{array}{r}3\\\times7\\\hline\end{array}$
$\begin{array}{r}2\\\times3\\\hline\end{array}$
$\begin{array}{r}4\\\times1\\\hline\end{array}$

F
$\begin{array}{r}3\\\times4\\\hline\end{array}$
$\begin{array}{r}2\\\times5\\\hline\end{array}$
$\begin{array}{r}1\\\times8\\\hline\end{array}$
$\begin{array}{r}8\\\times5\\\hline\end{array}$
$\begin{array}{r}6\\\times3\\\hline\end{array}$
$\begin{array}{r}5\\\times6\\\hline\end{array}$
$\begin{array}{r}9\\\times4\\\hline\end{array}$
$\begin{array}{r}2\\\times0\\\hline\end{array}$
$\begin{array}{r}9\\\times9\\\hline\end{array}$
$\begin{array}{r}1\\\times5\\\hline\end{array}$

G
$\begin{array}{r}8\\\times8\\\hline\end{array}$
$\begin{array}{r}0\\\times7\\\hline\end{array}$
$\begin{array}{r}9\\\times1\\\hline\end{array}$
$\begin{array}{r}3\\\times9\\\hline\end{array}$
$\begin{array}{r}6\\\times1\\\hline\end{array}$
$\begin{array}{r}4\\\times8\\\hline\end{array}$
$\begin{array}{r}0\\\times3\\\hline\end{array}$
$\begin{array}{r}5\\\times3\\\hline\end{array}$
$\begin{array}{r}7\\\times8\\\hline\end{array}$
$\begin{array}{r}6\\\times6\\\hline\end{array}$

H
$\begin{array}{r}4\\\times0\\\hline\end{array}$
$\begin{array}{r}3\\\times6\\\hline\end{array}$
$\begin{array}{r}2\\\times2\\\hline\end{array}$
$\begin{array}{r}7\\\times1\\\hline\end{array}$
$\begin{array}{r}0\\\times5\\\hline\end{array}$
$\begin{array}{r}9\\\times7\\\hline\end{array}$
$\begin{array}{r}4\\\times4\\\hline\end{array}$
$\begin{array}{r}1\\\times9\\\hline\end{array}$
$\begin{array}{r}3\\\times1\\\hline\end{array}$
$\begin{array}{r}8\\\times7\\\hline\end{array}$

I
$\begin{array}{r}2\\\times6\\\hline\end{array}$
$\begin{array}{r}7\\\times4\\\hline\end{array}$
$\begin{array}{r}5\\\times5\\\hline\end{array}$
$\begin{array}{r}0\\\times0\\\hline\end{array}$
$\begin{array}{r}8\\\times4\\\hline\end{array}$
$\begin{array}{r}5\\\times8\\\hline\end{array}$
$\begin{array}{r}1\\\times0\\\hline\end{array}$
$\begin{array}{r}8\\\times1\\\hline\end{array}$
$\begin{array}{r}6\\\times0\\\hline\end{array}$
$\begin{array}{r}9\\\times2\\\hline\end{array}$

J
$\begin{array}{r}6\\\times5\\\hline\end{array}$
$\begin{array}{r}1\\\times4\\\hline\end{array}$
$\begin{array}{r}5\\\times2\\\hline\end{array}$
$\begin{array}{r}4\\\times9\\\hline\end{array}$
$\begin{array}{r}7\\\times7\\\hline\end{array}$
$\begin{array}{r}2\\\times9\\\hline\end{array}$
$\begin{array}{r}7\\\times0\\\hline\end{array}$
$\begin{array}{r}6\\\times9\\\hline\end{array}$
$\begin{array}{r}3\\\times0\\\hline\end{array}$
$\begin{array}{r}4\\\times7\\\hline\end{array}$

8

Name _____

Minutes

1	2	3	4	5	6

Score

A	9 × 1 =	5 × 8 =	2 × 5 =	7 × 5 =	4 × 7 =
B	0 × 5 =	8 × 0 =	8 × 6 =	0 × 9 =	6 × 3 =
C	9 × 6 =	7 × 4 =	7 × 0 =	4 × 4 =	0 × 3 =
D	6 × 4 =	1 × 7 =	3 × 7 =	3 × 1 =	5 × 3 =
E	9 × 9 =	9 × 3 =	0 × 4 =	7 × 9 =	6 × 0 =
F	1 × 3 =	4 × 8 =	5 × 7 =	5 × 2 =	2 × 1 =
G	9 × 4 =	1 × 0 =	7 × 1 =	0 × 0 =	3 × 6 =
H	4 × 3 =	7 × 8 =	2 × 4 =	8 × 5 =	1 × 2 =
I	3 × 8 =	9 × 8 =	5 × 1 =	3 × 0 =	7 × 3 =
J	8 × 1 =	5 × 6 =	2 × 0 =	6 × 2 =	0 × 8 =
K	9 × 7 =	0 × 1 =	6 × 6 =	1 × 6 =	2 × 9 =
L	5 × 0 =	6 × 9 =	3 × 2 =	8 × 9 =	4 × 0 =
M	7 × 2 =	2 × 6 =	0 × 7 =	3 × 5 =	4 × 6 =
N	2 × 3 =	5 × 9 =	4 × 2 =	1 × 1 =	7 × 7 =
O	6 × 5 =	0 × 6 =	5 × 5 =	9 × 2 =	8 × 2 =
P	3 × 9 =	6 × 1 =	1 × 5 =	2 × 8 =	2 × 2 =
Q	1 × 4 =	1 × 9 =	4 × 9 =	0 × 2 =	6 × 7 =
R	8 × 4 =	4 × 5 =	7 × 6 =	9 × 5 =	5 × 4 =
S	8 × 8 =	6 × 8 =	9 × 0 =	3 × 3 =	8 × 7 =
T	3 × 4 =	4 × 1 =	2 × 7 =	8 × 3 =	1 × 8 =

Name _____

Minutes

1	2	3	4	5	6

Score

A	7 × 6 =	4 × 6 =	2 × 5 =	0 × 8 =	5 × 7 =
B	1 × 5 =	8 × 9 =	8 × 2 =	7 × 1 =	2 × 4 =
C	6 × 7 =	0 × 4 =	6 × 1 =	4 × 9 =	9 × 2 =
D	5 × 6 =	6 × 3 =	2 × 0 =	3 × 8 =	0 × 7 =
E	9 × 6 =	4 × 2 =	9 × 9 =	5 × 0 =	3 × 3 =
F	1 × 2 =	7 × 5 =	2 × 9 =	1 × 3 =	4 × 5 =
G	6 × 0 =	3 × 7 =	0 × 1 =	7 × 9 =	1 × 9 =
H	3 × 4 =	4 × 8 =	6 × 6 =	2 × 3 =	5 × 5 =
I	2 × 8 =	7 × 0 =	8 × 5 =	4 × 1 =	7 × 4 =
J	9 × 0 =	1 × 1 =	3 × 2 =	6 × 9 =	6 × 2 =
K	8 × 6 =	8 × 1 =	5 × 1 =	0 × 3 =	1 × 4 =
L	5 × 3 =	2 × 2 =	4 × 0 =	4 × 4 =	8 × 8 =
M	0 × 0 =	8 × 4 =	6 × 5 =	2 × 7 =	3 × 6 =
N	9 × 5 =	3 × 1 =	0 × 6 =	7 × 8 =	1 × 8 =
O	3 × 9 =	7 × 2 =	8 × 0 =	2 × 1 =	0 × 2 =
P	9 × 8 =	1 × 0 =	9 × 1 =	5 × 9 =	7 × 3 =
Q	6 × 4 =	9 × 7 =	1 × 7 =	9 × 3 =	5 × 4 =
R	7 × 7 =	0 × 5 =	5 × 8 =	3 × 0 =	6 × 8 =
S	9 × 4 =	4 × 3 =	8 × 7 =	0 × 9 =	3 × 5 =
T	1 × 6 =	5 × 2 =	2 × 6 =	4 × 7 =	8 × 3 =

Name _____

Minutes

1	2	3	4	5	6

Score

A	5)5	3)6	3)15	1)0	2)6	1)3	4)8	2)4	2)8	4)20
B	4)20	3)12	1)2	4)4	2)10	3)6	3)3	5)25	3)15	5)20
C	2)4	5)15	1)1	5)5	3)0	2)2	4)20	1)4	4)16	2)0
D	3)15	1)5	4)16	5)0	1)1	3)3	2)8	2)10	1)3	4)0
E	5)20	3)0	1)2	4)12	5)10	4)16	3)9	5)25	2)8	5)15
F	4)0	2)6	4)12	3)12	3)15	4)8	1)5	2)2	2)10	5)20
G	5)5	4)16	5)25	3)3	1)0	1)2	3)9	1)3	4)0	5)15
H	3)12	2)0	1)5	3)3	5)25	1)4	4)8	3)9	5)10	2)8
I	3)12	5)5	2)6	2)4	4)4	3)6	5)0	2)2	5)15	2)10
J	4)4	1)1	3)9	4)12	2)4	1)4	4)8	3)0	5)10	2)0

Name _____

Minutes

| 1 | 2 | 3 | 4 | 5 | 6 |

Score

	A	B	C	D	E	F	G	H	I	J
A	4)4	3)12	2)6	1)0	5)10	4)8	2)2	3)9	4)12	5)15
B	3)6	5)10	1)1	1)3	3)3	2)6	4)20	3)9	1)3	3)12
C	2)4	1)5	4)12	4)4	4)16	5)25	2)6	2)10	5)15	3)0
D	2)8	5)20	5)15	4)12	2)2	1)3	5)0	3)15	1)1	4)16
E	4)20	1)4	4)0	3)3	1)2	3)15	4)4	5)5	3)9	2)10
F	5)10	4)20	4)8	5)20	2)4	1)0	2)6	5)15	2)0	4)16
G	4)8	3)0	1)4	5)25	2)0	4)16	3)6	5)5	1)4	4)4
H	5)10	2)4	1)2	3)12	5)5	2)8	4)20	3)15	5)20	2)2
I	5)25	5)5	3)12	3)6	1)2	1)1	4)0	2)10	5)25	1)5
J	3)3	5)0	2)10	2)2	4)12	4)8	2)8	1)5	3)6	5)20

14

Name _____

Minutes						Score
1	2	3	4	5	6	

A	1⟌4	6⟌6	5⟌35	2⟌12	5⟌10	3⟌6	3⟌12	7⟌21	6⟌12	2⟌2
B	5⟌35	7⟌28	3⟌3	3⟌15	5⟌0	4⟌16	6⟌36	5⟌20	1⟌7	4⟌24
C	4⟌12	6⟌24	2⟌6	7⟌42	4⟌28	3⟌21	4⟌4	2⟌0	7⟌14	1⟌1
D	2⟌4	1⟌0	4⟌12	2⟌4	6⟌30	7⟌28	4⟌4	5⟌25	5⟌10	6⟌24
E	4⟌24	5⟌15	3⟌12	7⟌7	6⟌18	1⟌3	4⟌20	5⟌30	2⟌8	7⟌0
F	2⟌14	7⟌21	6⟌12	1⟌6	3⟌9	2⟌14	4⟌0	7⟌49	3⟌18	2⟌2
G	6⟌0	3⟌18	4⟌8	2⟌10	7⟌49	5⟌15	4⟌20	5⟌5	7⟌35	1⟌6
H	7⟌42	3⟌15	1⟌5	6⟌30	7⟌7	4⟌28	6⟌6	7⟌14	3⟌3	2⟌10
I	6⟌42	2⟌6	5⟌25	5⟌5	3⟌0	1⟌7	1⟌2	4⟌16	3⟌21	5⟌30
J	1⟌5	7⟌35	2⟌12	3⟌6	4⟌8	5⟌20	2⟌8	6⟌18	3⟌9	6⟌36

Minutes

1	2	3	4	5	6

Score

A	4)8	7)49	3)18	5)15	1)5	6)24	5)35	1)4	7)21	3)6
B	6)18	2)8	7)7	4)24	6)36	1)1	5)10	7)35	3)15	4)16
C	1)6	5)5	4)12	7)0	4)28	5)30	6)12	3)3	2)4	6)30
D	4)16	7)42	3)6	5)20	2)12	6)6	2)6	3)12	7)28	3)21
E	5)25	1)6	5)0	6)36	1)3	3)9	7)14	4)4	3)18	6)42
F	2)2	5)10	7)21	2)10	4)20	6)30	3)3	6)0	4)12	2)14
G	2)14	5)30	6)12	4)0	7)35	1)7	2)6	5)15	1)5	7)49
H	6)24	2)2	3)12	5)5	1)2	3)0	6)18	4)8	7)7	2)10
I	4)28	6)6	2)4	5)25	3)15	7)28	1)0	4)20	6)42	3)21
J	5)35	2)8	7)14	3)9	4)4	5)20	2)12	7)42	2)0	4)24

Name _____

Minutes

1	2	3	4	5	6

Score

A	3)27	4)12	7)14	2)8	9)63	3)6	5)10	3)9	8)48	3)15
B	1)3	5)25	7)0	2)16	6)36	2)12	4)24	9)36	3)24	8)16
C	5)40	1)7	9)18	2)2	6)0	9)81	8)56	4)4	5)45	6)18
D	3)9	8)32	1)0	6)48	4)16	7)35	1)6	5)5	9)0	2)18
E	6)30	2)10	4)0	8)72	1)5	9)54	3)3	5)20	2)6	7)49
F	4)36	8)0	7)14	6)12	7)63	8)48	7)7	3)18	9)81	3)12
G	7)28	2)16	9)9	1)5	4)16	5)0	8)24	1)2	4)28	6)42
H	5)15	2)4	7)42	1)1	8)8	9)36	4)32	9)27	5)30	1)9
I	3)21	9)45	4)20	7)56	2)0	8)64	5)15	6)54	4)8	6)24
J	6)6	1)8	5)35	8)40	6)30	3)0	9)72	2)14	7)21	1)4

Name _____

Minutes

1	2	3	4	5	6

Score

A	9)63	6)24	4)4	9)18	1)7	8)32	5)15	3)12	1)8	2)16
B	8)64	4)36	1)2	7)0	5)30	3)24	3)18	9)54	2)6	7)35
C	2)12	5)20	6)48	8)8	3)6	7)56	5)0	1)1	9)45	4)16
D	8)24	5)40	2)2	9)27	6)42	1)4	7)14	4)24	9)9	3)0
E	7)63	3)15	7)21	6)18	4)32	8)0	5)20	2)4	7)28	1)6
F	3)21	9)36	1)0	6)6	5)35	4)12	9)72	2)10	6)12	8)56
G	6)54	4)0	8)32	3)3	2)18	8)40	5)5	7)49	1)8	6)12
H	4)20	9)36	2)8	9)0	6)30	1)3	8)48	7)7	3)9	5)25
I	5)10	4)28	7)21	1)9	8)16	4)28	3)27	6)36	2)0	9)81
J	7)42	1)5	3)24	2)16	5)45	8)64	2)14	6)0	8)72	4)8

Name _____

Minutes

1	2	3	4	5	6

Score

A	$6\overline{)18}$	$1\overline{)6}$	$9\overline{)36}$	$3\overline{)18}$	$9\overline{)72}$	$6\overline{)36}$	$2\overline{)2}$	$9\overline{)63}$	$4\overline{)24}$	$8\overline{)32}$
B	$3\overline{)6}$	$5\overline{)30}$	$1\overline{)2}$	$8\overline{)56}$	$3\overline{)9}$	$2\overline{)10}$	$6\overline{)0}$	$5\overline{)45}$	$9\overline{)9}$	$4\overline{)8}$
C	$3\overline{)0}$	$8\overline{)16}$	$7\overline{)56}$	$3\overline{)24}$	$5\overline{)15}$	$4\overline{)36}$	$1\overline{)1}$	$7\overline{)42}$	$2\overline{)8}$	$6\overline{)54}$
D	$4\overline{)16}$	$5\overline{)20}$	$2\overline{)18}$	$7\overline{)7}$	$5\overline{)0}$	$1\overline{)7}$	$4\overline{)4}$	$9\overline{)27}$	$7\overline{)21}$	$2\overline{)0}$
E	$6\overline{)42}$	$2\overline{)4}$	$6\overline{)36}$	$1\overline{)5}$	$5\overline{)25}$	$9\overline{)54}$	$3\overline{)15}$	$7\overline{)35}$	$6\overline{)12}$	$5\overline{)5}$
F	$4\overline{)32}$	$7\overline{)28}$	$3\overline{)3}$	$6\overline{)30}$	$2\overline{)12}$	$5\overline{)40}$	$4\overline{)0}$	$6\overline{)30}$	$1\overline{)4}$	$8\overline{)48}$
G	$9\overline{)18}$	$2\overline{)16}$	$9\overline{)0}$	$4\overline{)12}$	$6\overline{)6}$	$1\overline{)0}$	$8\overline{)24}$	$3\overline{)27}$	$7\overline{)49}$	$4\overline{)12}$
H	$7\overline{)14}$	$5\overline{)10}$	$9\overline{)72}$	$1\overline{)9}$	$8\overline{)8}$	$6\overline{)48}$	$3\overline{)12}$	$8\overline{)56}$	$8\overline{)72}$	$4\overline{)20}$
I	$1\overline{)3}$	$8\overline{)40}$	$6\overline{)24}$	$1\overline{)2}$	$5\overline{)20}$	$9\overline{)81}$	$2\overline{)14}$	$7\overline{)0}$	$3\overline{)6}$	$9\overline{)45}$
J	$7\overline{)63}$	$3\overline{)21}$	$5\overline{)35}$	$2\overline{)6}$	$8\overline{)0}$	$4\overline{)28}$	$6\overline{)54}$	$1\overline{)8}$	$8\overline{)64}$	$7\overline{)42}$

Name _____

Minutes

1	2	3	4	5	6

Score

A	5)10	4)28	2)4	9)63	6)30	4)16	9)0	3)15	8)72	6)18
B	8)48	3)6	7)21	1)3	7)56	6)0	2)16	6)54	1)7	9)45
C	7)49	5)35	3)24	7)7	3)12	8)24	1)1	9)72	7)35	5)25
D	9)27	1)0	8)40	5)15	2)2	6)48	5)0	4)24	2)8	5)15
E	7)49	6)12	3)3	2)12	9)9	1)5	6)24	4)4	8)64	5)45
F	2)6	6)24	4)12	3)0	8)8	4)36	2)0	7)28	9)63	3)21
G	6)42	7)35	1)8	9)54	3)27	4)0	5)5	5)40	1)4	7)0
H	4)32	2)18	9)81	8)56	3)9	1)3	2)14	9)36	4)8	8)16
I	7)14	8)48	5)20	6)6	1)2	8)0	5)30	8)56	1)9	8)32
J	1)6	6)54	6)36	3)18	7)63	4)8	2)10	7)42	9)18	4)20

Name _____

Minutes

1	2	3	4	5	6

Score

A	5)‾20	3)‾6	8)‾16	4)‾32	9)‾9	2)‾10	4)‾20	7)‾56	3)‾21	7)‾35
B	8)‾72	6)‾18	2)‾6	7)‾0	5)‾45	4)‾24	8)‾8	1)‾5	7)‾49	6)‾36
C	6)‾0	4)‾16	1)‾2	6)‾54	5)‾15	2)‾16	1)‾8	8)‾48	4)‾8	5)‾15
D	3)‾9	7)‾14	6)‾30	3)‾18	4)‾0	9)‾63	1)‾1	9)‾45	5)‾30	2)‾2
E	8)‾24	2)‾8	7)‾42	1)‾7	6)‾48	3)‾27	2)‾0	7)‾28	5)‾5	9)‾27
F	2)‾14	8)‾64	4)‾28	5)‾40	1)‾6	3)‾3	4)‾32	6)‾12	3)‾15	8)‾40
G	9)‾0	4)‾12	2)‾4	7)‾7	5)‾0	1)‾9	7)‾63	4)‾20	8)‾0	1)‾4
H	1)‾3	9)‾81	6)‾24	5)‾10	8)‾64	7)‾49	3)‾24	9)‾18	6)‾42	8)‾32
I	7)‾21	9)‾36	3)‾0	9)‾72	2)‾12	7)‾21	5)‾25	6)‾30	4)‾4	9)‾54
J	5)‾35	2)‾18	9)‾27	8)‾32	4)‾36	6)‾6	1)‾0	3)‾12	5)‾40	8)‾56

Name _____

Minutes

1	2	3	4	5	6

Score

A	8√40	3√27	7√42	8√48	3√3	8√24	7√14	2√10	6√36	9√81
B	6√42	4√32	1√4	9√45	5√10	3√15	5√40	4√4	1√3	9√27
C	7√49	6√6	2√4	7√63	4√12	2√0	7√35	6√18	8√0	2√14
D	1√0	9√72	3√24	4√0	7√7	6√54	1√8	9√18	4√28	5√20
E	8√16	5√30	1√9	8√72	6√24	2√18	5√5	7√56	3√12	3√0
F	2√12	9√0	4√20	3√6	6√36	7√0	2√2	8√56	1√6	7√28
G	5√15	7√28	3√18	5√0	1√2	4√36	6√12	4√8	8√8	6√48
H	8√48	1√5	7√49	4√32	5√40	6√0	2√16	6√18	9√63	2√8
I	9√54	7√21	9√63	1√8	8√32	5√25	9√9	4√16	3√21	4√24
J	5√35	3√9	9√36	8√64	5√45	2√6	5√25	1√1	6√30	4√16

22

Name _____

Minutes

1	2	3	4	5	6

Score

A	36 ÷ 6 =	8 ÷ 1 =	45 ÷ 9 =	16 ÷ 8 =	35 ÷ 5 =
B	24 ÷ 8 =	27 ÷ 9 =	20 ÷ 5 =	21 ÷ 3 =	8 ÷ 2 =
C	20 ÷ 4 =	42 ÷ 7 =	18 ÷ 6 =	14 ÷ 2 =	28 ÷ 7 =
D	56 ÷ 8 =	9 ÷ 3 =	3 ÷ 1 =	40 ÷ 8 =	12 ÷ 4 =
E	10 ÷ 2 =	48 ÷ 6 =	45 ÷ 5 =	0 ÷ 6 =	15 ÷ 3 =
F	7 ÷ 7 =	6 ÷ 2 =	18 ÷ 9 =	7 ÷ 1 =	32 ÷ 4 =
G	5 ÷ 1 =	35 ÷ 5 =	56 ÷ 7 =	5 ÷ 5 =	30 ÷ 6 =
H	18 ÷ 6 =	15 ÷ 5 =	18 ÷ 2 =	72 ÷ 8 =	2 ÷ 1 =
I	30 ÷ 5 =	1 ÷ 1 =	21 ÷ 7 =	8 ÷ 4 =	0 ÷ 3 =
J	9 ÷ 9 =	28 ÷ 4 =	16 ÷ 4 =	12 ÷ 2 =	36 ÷ 9 =
K	8 ÷ 8 =	27 ÷ 3 =	6 ÷ 6 =	6 ÷ 3 =	0 ÷ 4 =
L	12 ÷ 3 =	81 ÷ 9 =	0 ÷ 2 =	49 ÷ 7 =	36 ÷ 9 =
M	30 ÷ 6 =	32 ÷ 8 =	9 ÷ 1 =	0 ÷ 8 =	14 ÷ 7 =
N	35 ÷ 7 =	16 ÷ 2 =	0 ÷ 7 =	42 ÷ 6 =	6 ÷ 1 =
O	45 ÷ 9 =	24 ÷ 4 =	10 ÷ 5 =	0 ÷ 1 =	12 ÷ 6 =
P	2 ÷ 2 =	0 ÷ 5 =	24 ÷ 6 =	40 ÷ 5 =	24 ÷ 3 =
Q	54 ÷ 6 =	27 ÷ 9 =	18 ÷ 3 =	25 ÷ 5 =	63 ÷ 9 =
R	64 ÷ 8 =	4 ÷ 1 =	4 ÷ 4 =	0 ÷ 9 =	4 ÷ 2 =
S	72 ÷ 8 =	63 ÷ 7 =	48 ÷ 8 =	72 ÷ 9 =	24 ÷ 8 =
T	36 ÷ 4 =	54 ÷ 9 =	3 ÷ 3 =	40 ÷ 5 =	14 ÷ 7 =

Name _____

Minutes

1	2	3	4	5	6

Score

A	32 ÷ 8 =	64 ÷ 8 =	4 ÷ 2 =	36 ÷ 6 =	35 ÷ 5 =
B	48 ÷ 6 =	9 ÷ 3 =	18 ÷ 6 =	16 ÷ 2 =	56 ÷ 7 =
C	27 ÷ 9 =	63 ÷ 7 =	48 ÷ 8 =	9 ÷ 9 =	21 ÷ 3 =
D	10 ÷ 2 =	36 ÷ 9 =	4 ÷ 1 =	24 ÷ 4 =	81 ÷ 9 =
E	40 ÷ 5 =	42 ÷ 7 =	54 ÷ 6 =	2 ÷ 2 =	21 ÷ 7 =
F	49 ÷ 7 =	6 ÷ 1 =	8 ÷ 4 =	10 ÷ 5 =	16 ÷ 4 =
G	72 ÷ 8 =	12 ÷ 6 =	8 ÷ 1 =	12 ÷ 4 =	3 ÷ 1 =
H	24 ÷ 3 =	20 ÷ 5 =	16 ÷ 8 =	0 ÷ 1 =	56 ÷ 7 =
I	27 ÷ 9 =	32 ÷ 4 =	0 ÷ 3 =	63 ÷ 9 =	40 ÷ 8 =
J	0 ÷ 7 =	1 ÷ 1 =	14 ÷ 7 =	6 ÷ 3 =	14 ÷ 2 =
K	30 ÷ 6 =	12 ÷ 3 =	64 ÷ 8 =	49 ÷ 7 =	0 ÷ 6 =
L	8 ÷ 8 =	42 ÷ 6 =	0 ÷ 2 =	5 ÷ 5 =	28 ÷ 4 =
M	45 ÷ 9 =	35 ÷ 7 =	4 ÷ 4 =	8 ÷ 2 =	24 ÷ 8 =
N	0 ÷ 4 =	12 ÷ 2 =	30 ÷ 5 =	12 ÷ 4 =	18 ÷ 3 =
O	32 ÷ 8 =	6 ÷ 6 =	27 ÷ 3 =	0 ÷ 9 =	45 ÷ 5 =
P	5 ÷ 1 =	15 ÷ 5 =	2 ÷ 1 =	3 ÷ 3 =	42 ÷ 6 =
Q	7 ÷ 7 =	56 ÷ 8 =	18 ÷ 2 =	0 ÷ 5 =	7 ÷ 1 =
R	72 ÷ 9 =	20 ÷ 4 =	0 ÷ 8 =	36 ÷ 4 =	36 ÷ 6 =
S	25 ÷ 5 =	9 ÷ 1 =	28 ÷ 4 =	54 ÷ 9 =	28 ÷ 7 =
T	15 ÷ 3 =	18 ÷ 9 =	24 ÷ 6 =	6 ÷ 2 =	45 ÷ 9 =

Name _____

Minutes

| 1 | 2 | 3 | 4 | 5 | 6 |

Score

A
$\begin{array}{r}5\\\times0\end{array}$
$\begin{array}{r}4\\\times1\end{array}$
$\begin{array}{r}2\\\times6\end{array}$
$5\overline{)25}$
$\begin{array}{r}7\\\times3\end{array}$
$4\overline{)28}$
$\begin{array}{r}5\\\times7\end{array}$
$3\overline{)3}$
$\begin{array}{r}1\\\times7\end{array}$
$7\overline{)28}$

B
$2\overline{)14}$
$\begin{array}{r}8\\\times2\end{array}$
$\begin{array}{r}3\\\times2\end{array}$
$7\overline{)21}$
$\begin{array}{r}0\\\times6\end{array}$
$\begin{array}{r}8\\\times8\end{array}$
$5\overline{)10}$
$\begin{array}{r}4\\\times2\end{array}$
$9\overline{)81}$
$9\overline{)36}$

C
$4\overline{)32}$
$\begin{array}{r}6\\\times3\end{array}$
$\begin{array}{r}5\\\times9\end{array}$
$3\overline{)0}$
$2\overline{)12}$
$\begin{array}{r}2\\\times1\end{array}$
$\begin{array}{r}8\\\times0\end{array}$
$8\overline{)48}$
$\begin{array}{r}3\\\times5\end{array}$
$\begin{array}{r}7\\\times9\end{array}$

D
$6\overline{)42}$
$\begin{array}{r}1\\\times4\end{array}$
$\begin{array}{r}3\\\times0\end{array}$
$7\overline{)0}$
$\begin{array}{r}5\\\times3\end{array}$
$6\overline{)24}$
$\begin{array}{r}0\\\times2\end{array}$
$\begin{array}{r}6\\\times5\end{array}$
$\begin{array}{r}9\\\times3\end{array}$
$5\overline{)5}$

E
$2\overline{)2}$
$\begin{array}{r}3\\\times6\end{array}$
$\begin{array}{r}9\\\times7\end{array}$
$\begin{array}{r}3\\\times1\end{array}$
$6\overline{)30}$
$1\overline{)0}$
$\begin{array}{r}7\\\times7\end{array}$
$\begin{array}{r}0\\\times9\end{array}$
$3\overline{)6}$
$\begin{array}{r}8\\\times5\end{array}$

F
$\begin{array}{r}2\\\times0\end{array}$
$5\overline{)5}$
$4\overline{)12}$
$\begin{array}{r}6\\\times0\end{array}$
$\begin{array}{r}1\\\times1\end{array}$
$1\overline{)7}$
$9\overline{)18}$
$\begin{array}{r}5\\\times4\end{array}$
$8\overline{)24}$
$\begin{array}{r}1\\\times9\end{array}$

G
$\begin{array}{r}9\\\times1\end{array}$
$\begin{array}{r}6\\\times6\end{array}$
$\begin{array}{r}0\\\times4\end{array}$
$9\overline{)72}$
$2\overline{)4}$
$\begin{array}{r}4\\\times4\end{array}$
$5\overline{)45}$
$7\overline{)42}$
$\begin{array}{r}2\\\times8\end{array}$
$\begin{array}{r}7\\\times0\end{array}$

H
$3\overline{)24}$
$\begin{array}{r}5\\\times2\end{array}$
$8\overline{)32}$
$\begin{array}{r}3\\\times3\end{array}$
$5\overline{)0}$
$1\overline{)6}$
$\begin{array}{r}0\\\times8\end{array}$
$3\overline{)12}$
$8\overline{)40}$
$\begin{array}{r}6\\\times9\end{array}$

I
$\begin{array}{r}7\\\times5\end{array}$
$4\overline{)24}$
$7\overline{)14}$
$\begin{array}{r}9\\\times6\end{array}$
$\begin{array}{r}2\\\times4\end{array}$
$1\overline{)8}$
$9\overline{)27}$
$\begin{array}{r}4\\\times0\end{array}$
$\begin{array}{r}1\\\times0\end{array}$
$8\overline{)56}$

J
$2\overline{)18}$
$\begin{array}{r}1\\\times8\end{array}$
$\begin{array}{r}9\\\times0\end{array}$
$6\overline{)6}$
$\begin{array}{r}9\\\times8\end{array}$
$\begin{array}{r}8\\\times7\end{array}$
$4\overline{)36}$
$\begin{array}{r}0\\\times1\end{array}$
$\begin{array}{r}4\\\times5\end{array}$
$6\overline{)48}$

Name _____

Minutes

1	2	3	4	5	6

Score

A $\begin{array}{r}2\\ \times 4\\ \hline\end{array}$ $\begin{array}{r}9\\ \times 0\\ \hline\end{array}$ $1\overline{)5}$ $8\overline{)56}$ $\begin{array}{r}1\\ \times 5\\ \hline\end{array}$ $\begin{array}{r}8\\ \times 0\\ \hline\end{array}$ $8\overline{)72}$ $8\overline{)16}$ $\begin{array}{r}3\\ \times 5\\ \hline\end{array}$ $\begin{array}{r}8\\ \times 7\\ \hline\end{array}$

B $\begin{array}{r}0\\ \times 0\\ \hline\end{array}$ $\begin{array}{r}7\\ \times 3\\ \hline\end{array}$ $\begin{array}{r}4\\ \times 9\\ \hline\end{array}$ $6\overline{)0}$ $\begin{array}{r}1\\ \times 0\\ \hline\end{array}$ $\begin{array}{r}6\\ \times 6\\ \hline\end{array}$ $\begin{array}{r}0\\ \times 4\\ \hline\end{array}$ $\begin{array}{r}8\\ \times 3\\ \hline\end{array}$ $2\overline{)2}$ $9\overline{)27}$

C $6\overline{)54}$ $\begin{array}{r}0\\ \times 1\\ \hline\end{array}$ $3\overline{)9}$ $6\overline{)12}$ $\begin{array}{r}3\\ \times 6\\ \hline\end{array}$ $\begin{array}{r}4\\ \times 1\\ \hline\end{array}$ $5\overline{)30}$ $\begin{array}{r}5\\ \times 2\\ \hline\end{array}$ $2\overline{)12}$ $\begin{array}{r}4\\ \times 7\\ \hline\end{array}$

D $\begin{array}{r}5\\ \times 8\\ \hline\end{array}$ $5\overline{)35}$ $\begin{array}{r}4\\ \times 0\\ \hline\end{array}$ $9\overline{)45}$ $\begin{array}{r}7\\ \times 4\\ \hline\end{array}$ $\begin{array}{r}2\\ \times 2\\ \hline\end{array}$ $4\overline{)12}$ $\begin{array}{r}9\\ \times 3\\ \hline\end{array}$ $\begin{array}{r}1\\ \times 6\\ \hline\end{array}$ $3\overline{)6}$

E $\begin{array}{r}1\\ \times 9\\ \hline\end{array}$ $1\overline{)2}$ $2\overline{)18}$ $\begin{array}{r}9\\ \times 7\\ \hline\end{array}$ $\begin{array}{r}0\\ \times 8\\ \hline\end{array}$ $4\overline{)4}$ $\begin{array}{r}3\\ \times 1\\ \hline\end{array}$ $5\overline{)0}$ $8\overline{)64}$ $\begin{array}{r}3\\ \times 8\\ \hline\end{array}$

F $\begin{array}{r}9\\ \times 5\\ \hline\end{array}$ $1\overline{)7}$ $\begin{array}{r}8\\ \times 2\\ \hline\end{array}$ $\begin{array}{r}2\\ \times 0\\ \hline\end{array}$ $4\overline{)32}$ $\begin{array}{r}6\\ \times 4\\ \hline\end{array}$ $3\overline{)18}$ $\begin{array}{r}2\\ \times 9\\ \hline\end{array}$ $3\overline{)12}$ $\begin{array}{r}7\\ \times 6\\ \hline\end{array}$

G $2\overline{)8}$ $\begin{array}{r}1\\ \times 3\\ \hline\end{array}$ $7\overline{)21}$ $\begin{array}{r}8\\ \times 5\\ \hline\end{array}$ $7\overline{)7}$ $\begin{array}{r}0\\ \times 2\\ \hline\end{array}$ $7\overline{)42}$ $7\overline{)35}$ $\begin{array}{r}4\\ \times 4\\ \hline\end{array}$ $6\overline{)24}$

H $\begin{array}{r}5\\ \times 0\\ \hline\end{array}$ $9\overline{)63}$ $\begin{array}{r}1\\ \times 8\\ \hline\end{array}$ $5\overline{)10}$ $1\overline{)1}$ $\begin{array}{r}7\\ \times 0\\ \hline\end{array}$ $8\overline{)32}$ $\begin{array}{r}5\\ \times 5\\ \hline\end{array}$ $\begin{array}{r}6\\ \times 9\\ \hline\end{array}$ $7\overline{)49}$

I $\begin{array}{r}3\\ \times 0\\ \hline\end{array}$ $9\overline{)0}$ $\begin{array}{r}6\\ \times 1\\ \hline\end{array}$ $9\overline{)72}$ $\begin{array}{r}0\\ \times 7\\ \hline\end{array}$ $2\overline{)6}$ $\begin{array}{r}9\\ \times 9\\ \hline\end{array}$ $\begin{array}{r}6\\ \times 0\\ \hline\end{array}$ $6\overline{)48}$ $\begin{array}{r}9\\ \times 1\\ \hline\end{array}$

J $\begin{array}{r}3\\ \times 3\\ \hline\end{array}$ $3\overline{)0}$ $\begin{array}{r}7\\ \times 2\\ \hline\end{array}$ $\begin{array}{r}5\\ \times 6\\ \hline\end{array}$ $1\overline{)8}$ $\begin{array}{r}6\\ \times 8\\ \hline\end{array}$ $5\overline{)20}$ $5\overline{)35}$ $\begin{array}{r}2\\ \times 7\\ \hline\end{array}$ $4\overline{)36}$

© Carson-Dellosa Publ. CD-0926

Name _____

Grade _____

SCORE SHEET

★ ★ ★ ★ ★ ★

Test No.	Factors/ Div. to:	Time	0-69	70	71	72	73	74	75	76	77	78	79	80	81	82	83	84	85	86	87	88	89	90	91	92	93	94	95	96	97	98	99	100

FAST FACTS AWARD

Presented to _____

For attaining 100% accuracy

within a _____ minute

time limit on the

"Beat It" _____ Facts Test.

Date _____   Signature _____

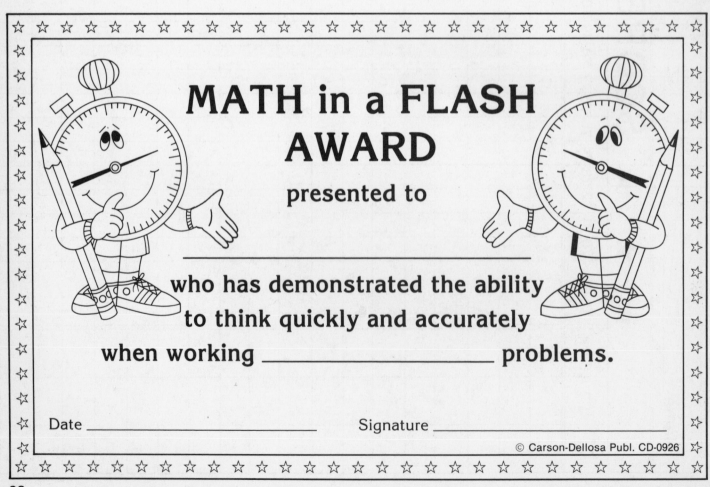

MATH in a FLASH AWARD

presented to

_____

who has demonstrated the ability

to think quickly and accurately

when working _____ problems.

Date _____   Signature _____

28

Name_____

Multiply to solve the problems. For every row you complete, mark an X on a base. Can you make a home run?

a. $\begin{array}{r} 1 \\ \times 1 \\ \hline \end{array}$ b. $\begin{array}{r} 4 \\ \times 0 \\ \hline \end{array}$ c. $\begin{array}{r} 1 \\ \times 2 \\ \hline \end{array}$ d. $\begin{array}{r} 5 \\ \times 2 \\ \hline \end{array}$ e. $\begin{array}{r} 3 \\ \times 5 \\ \hline \end{array}$

f. $\begin{array}{r} 2 \\ \times 2 \\ \hline \end{array}$ g. $\begin{array}{r} 1 \\ \times 5 \\ \hline \end{array}$ h. $\begin{array}{r} 2 \\ \times 3 \\ \hline \end{array}$ i. $\begin{array}{r} 3 \\ \times 0 \\ \hline \end{array}$ j. $\begin{array}{r} 5 \\ \times 1 \\ \hline \end{array}$

k. $\begin{array}{r} 2 \\ \times 4 \\ \hline \end{array}$ l. $\begin{array}{r} 1 \\ \times 3 \\ \hline \end{array}$ m. $\begin{array}{r} 5 \\ \times 3 \\ \hline \end{array}$ n. $\begin{array}{r} 0 \\ \times 1 \\ \hline \end{array}$ o. $\begin{array}{r} 2 \\ \times 1 \\ \hline \end{array}$

p. $\begin{array}{r} 1 \\ \times 4 \\ \hline \end{array}$ q. $\begin{array}{r} 5 \\ \times 5 \\ \hline \end{array}$ r. $\begin{array}{r} 3 \\ \times 4 \\ \hline \end{array}$ s. $\begin{array}{r} 0 \\ \times 5 \\ \hline \end{array}$ t. $\begin{array}{r} 3 \\ \times 3 \\ \hline \end{array}$

2nd

3rd   1st

H

29

Name_____

Multiply to solve the problems.

a. 4 ×3

b. 3 ×1

c. 2 ×2

d. 5 ×5

e. 0 ×3

f. 4 ×2

g. 1 ×5

h. 5 ×4

i. 2 ×5

j. 0 ×1

k. 2 ×3

l. 3 ×4

m. 4 ×4

n. 0 ×0

o. 5 ×2

p. 3 ×3

q. 4 ×0

r. 3 ×5

s. 1 ×1

30

© Carson-Dellosa Publ. CD-0926

Name _____

Multiply or divide to solve the problems and color:

0 = red   2 = yellow   5 = blue
1 = green   4 = orange

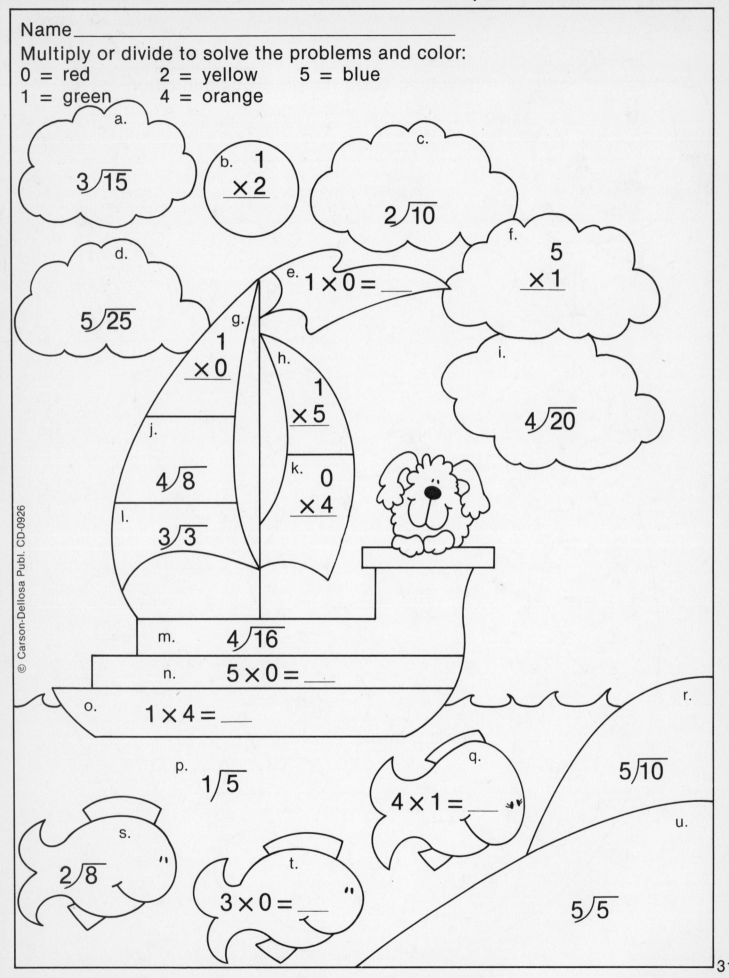

a. $3\overline{)15}$

b. $\begin{array}{r} 1 \\ \times 2 \\ \hline \end{array}$

c. $2\overline{)10}$

d. $5\overline{)25}$

e. $1 \times 0 = \underline{}$

f. $\begin{array}{r} 5 \\ \times 1 \\ \hline \end{array}$

g. $\begin{array}{r} 1 \\ \times 0 \\ \hline \end{array}$

h. $\begin{array}{r} 1 \\ \times 5 \\ \hline \end{array}$

i. $4\overline{)20}$

j. $4\overline{)8}$

k. $\begin{array}{r} 0 \\ \times 4 \\ \hline \end{array}$

l. $3\overline{)3}$

m. $4\overline{)16}$

n. $5 \times 0 = \underline{}$

o. $1 \times 4 = \underline{}$

p. $1\overline{)5}$

q. $4 \times 1 = \underline{}$

r. $5\overline{)10}$

s. $2\overline{)8}$

t. $3 \times 0 = \underline{}$

u. $5\overline{)5}$

© Carson-Dellosa Publ. CD-0926

Name_____

Divide to solve the problems and color:

0 = red	2 = green	4 = orange
1 = yellow	3 = blue	5 = purple

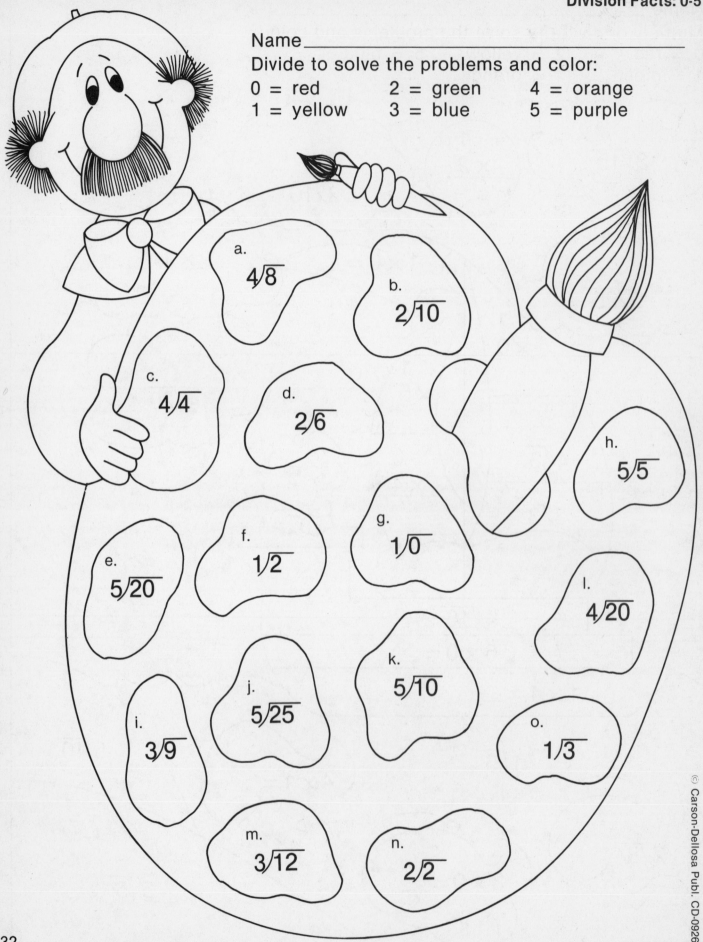

a. $4\overline{)8}$

b. $2\overline{)10}$

c. $4\overline{)4}$

d. $2\overline{)6}$

h. $5\overline{)5}$

e. $5\overline{)20}$

f. $1\overline{)2}$

g. $1\overline{)0}$

l. $4\overline{)20}$

i. $3\overline{)9}$

j. $5\overline{)25}$

k. $5\overline{)10}$

o. $1\overline{)3}$

m. $3\overline{)12}$

n. $2\overline{)2}$

Name _____

Minutes

1	2	3	4	5	6

Score

	3	7	1	6	0	5	9	2	7	4
A	×6	×2	×3	×7	×9	×4	×1	×6	×9	×5

	8	1	7	2	6	4	3	8	0	5
B	×1	×5	×0	×2	×0	×8	×2	×7	×3	×9

	5	9	4	0	6	0	7	4	5	2
C	×1	×3	×2	×8	×5	×1	×8	×4	×3	×0

	7	2	9	2	8	1	5	0	7	3
D	×6	×5	×2	×8	×4	×2	×8	×4	×4	×8

	6	1	3	8	2	7	3	6	1	6
E	×6	×0	×7	×6	×3	×1	×5	×9	×8	×4

	1	8	4	3	5	4	6	1	9	2
F	×6	×8	×7	×1	×2	×0	×2	×4	×0	×7

	5	0	8	2	9	0	4	5	3	8
G	×5	×7	×3	×1	×6	×2	×3	×7	×3	×9

	9	4	8	1	4	5	3	9	2	7
H	×8	×1	×0	×7	×6	×0	×9	×5	×4	×7

	0	6	3	7	1	8	0	9	6	8
I	×0	×8	×0	×3	×1	×5	×6	×7	×1	×2

	6	5	2	9	0	9	4	3	7	1
J	×3	×6	×9	×4	×5	×9	×9	×4	×5	×9

Name _____

Minutes

1	2	3	4	5	6

Score

A
7	4	3	9	1	8	2	6	0	5
×4	×6	×1	×5	×4	×4	×3	×8	×6	×5

B
8	4	0	4	3	6	7	1	8	2
×1	×0	×3	×3	×5	×3	×3	×0	×9	×7

C
5	2	8	0	5	4	1	9	3	6
×4	×0	×7	×0	×1	×7	×6	×1	×8	×0

D
7	4	2	6	9	0	5	7	1	3
×1	×9	×4	×7	×0	×7	×9	×6	×3	×4

E
0	8	3	5	1	9	5	2	6	4
×9	×5	×2	×6	×1	×4	×0	×2	×2	×5

F
7	3	1	8	6	4	2	8	0	5
×7	×9	×5	×0	×6	×1	×6	×3	×2	×2

G
9	1	7	4	0	5	9	2	8	3
×3	×9	×0	×4	×5	×8	×9	×1	×8	×0

H
2	6	6	1	7	4	0	9	3	7
×8	×1	×9	×7	×5	×8	×1	×8	×7	×9

I
5	0	6	3	5	2	8	7	1	9
×7	×8	×4	×3	×3	×9	×6	×2	×2	×7

J
8	3	0	7	2	9	1	9	4	6
×2	×6	×4	×8	×5	×2	×8	×6	×2	×5

Name _____

Multiply or divide to solve the problems and color:

0 = purple   3 = yellow
1 = orange   4 = red
2 = green   5 = blue

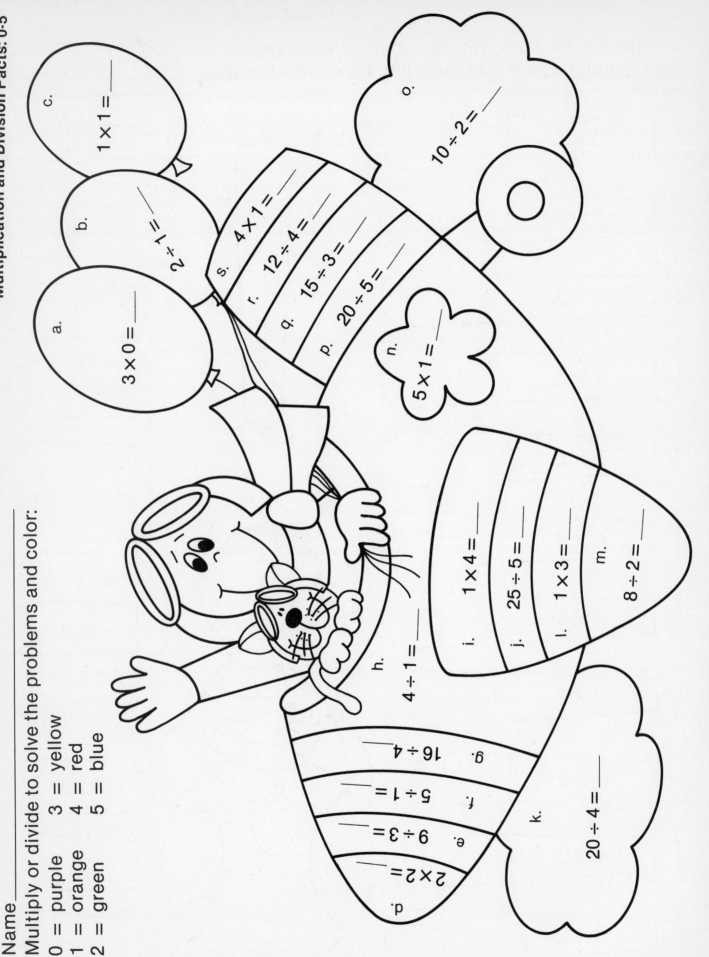

a.

$3 \times 0 =$ ___

b.

$2 \div 1 =$ ___

c.

$1 \times 1 =$ ___

o.

$10 \div 2 =$ ___

s.

$4 \times 1 =$ ___

r.

$12 \div 4 =$ ___

q.

$15 \div 3 =$ ___

p.

$20 \div 5 =$ ___

n.

$5 \times 1 =$ ___

h.

$4 \div 1 =$ ___

i.

$1 \times 4 =$ ___

j.

$25 \div 5 =$ ___

l.

$1 \times 3 =$ ___

m.

$8 \div 2 =$ ___

g.

$16 \div 4 =$ ___

f.

$5 \div 1 =$ ___

e.

$9 \div 3 =$ ___

d.

$2 \times 2 =$ ___

k.

$20 \div 4 =$ ___

Name_____

Multiply to solve the problems. Cut out each answer at the right of the page and paste it to the correct baseball bat.

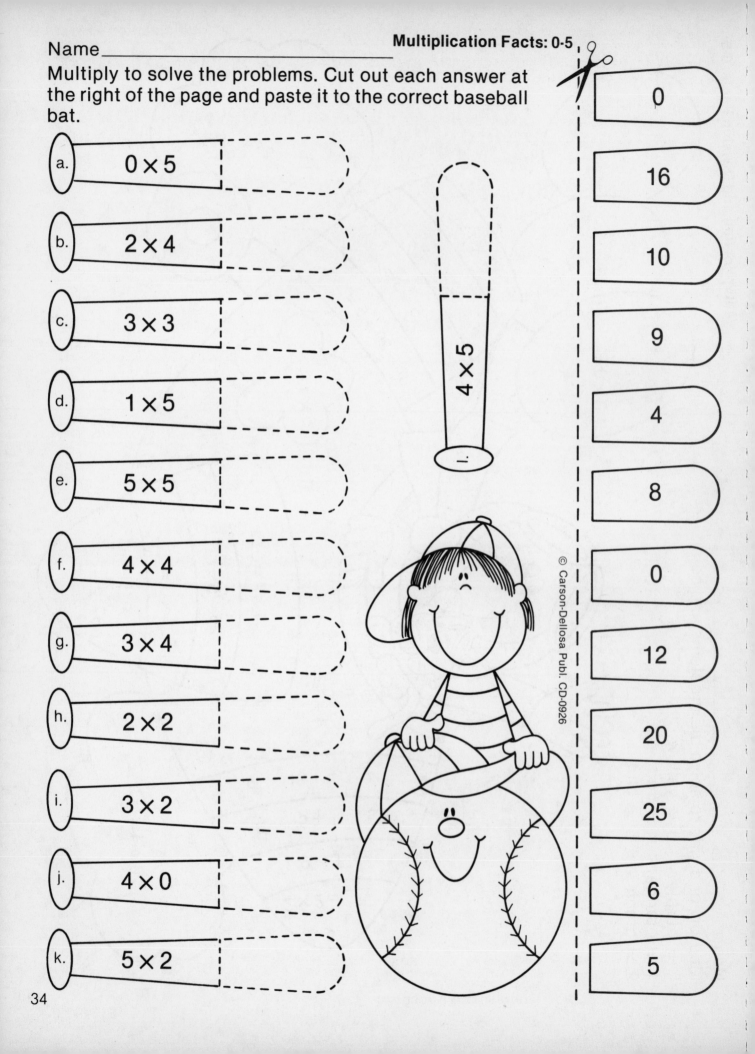

a. 0×5

b. 2×4

c. 3×3

d. 1×5

e. 5×5

f. 4×4

g. 3×4

h. 2×2

i. 3×2

j. 4×0

k. 5×2

l. 4×5

0

16

10

9

4

8

0

12

20

25

6

5

Name_____

Multiply to solve the problems in the problem list. Use × and = to find the same problems hidden in the puzzle. Circle each hidden problem.

Problem List

1 × 4 = _____
5 × 3 = _____
3 × 4 = _____
0 × 3 = _____
4 × 4 = _____
2 × 4 = _____
1 × 2 = _____
5 × 5 = _____
3 × 3 = _____
0 × 1 = _____
4 × 5 = _____
2 × 2 = _____
1 × 1 = _____
5 × 2 = _____
3 × 2 = _____
4 × 2 = _____
4 × 1 = _____
2 × 1 = _____

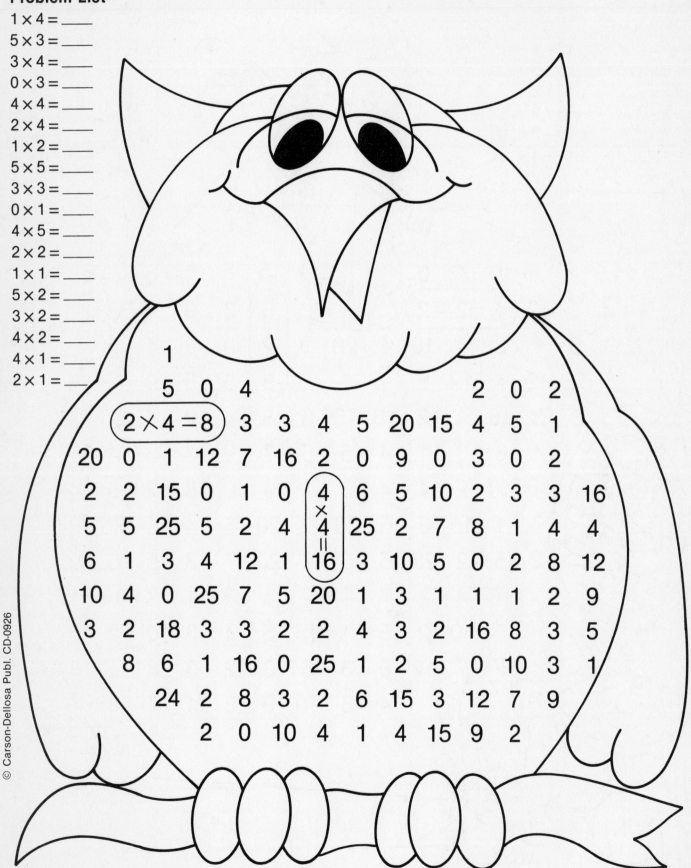

35

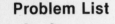Name_____

Divide to solve the problems in the problem list. Use ÷ and = to find the same problems hidden in the puzzle. Circle each hidden problem.

Problem List

3 ÷ 3 = ____	12 ÷ 4 = ____
15 ÷ 5 = ____	5 ÷ 5 = ____
20 ÷ 5 = ____	10 ÷ 5 = ____
25 ÷ 5 = ____	8 ÷ 2 = ____
10 ÷ 2 = ____	6 ÷ 3 = ____
8 ÷ 4 = ____	16 ÷ 4 = ____
9 ÷ 3 = ____	6 ÷ 2 = ____
20 ÷ 4 = ____	
15 ÷ 3 = ____	
4 ÷ 2 = ____	
12 ÷ 3 = ____	

```
        10  7   0              15   8
    12  (4 ÷ 2 = 2)           (6)  3   9   1
    6   1   3   4  10   4  20   9  (÷) 0   8   4   3
    12  12  4   12  5   1   1   2  (2) 5   5   2  15
    3   3   16  4   2   16 15   6  (=) 4   2   4  20
                                   (3)
    4   6   3   1   4   5   5   7   9   3   3   4   8
    16  10  2   4   4   3   1   9   0   8   2   5   4
    7   1  15   3   5  20   2  20   5   4   8  25   3
    2   5   2  25   5   5   7  20   7   3   5   5   9
        16  4   2   7   9   2   5   5   1   7   8   1
            10  2   5   1  15   5   4   3   0   2   5
                12  0   3   6   3   2   3   8   4   8
                    4   8  10   9   3   1   7   6
```

36

Name_____

Multiply to solve the problems. Don't "leaf" any blank.

a. $3 \times 4 =$ ___

b. $1 \times 3 =$ ___

c. $5 \times 5 =$ ___

d. $2 \times 4 =$ ___

e. $4 \times 1 =$ ___

f. $3 \times 2 =$ ___

g. $1 \times 0 =$ ___

h. $2 \times 7 =$ ___

i. $2 \times 5 =$ ___

j. $0 \times 3 =$ ___

k. $4 \times 5 =$ ___

l. $2 \times 1 =$ ___

m. $3 \times 5 =$ ___

n. $2 \times 3 =$ ___

o. $4 \times 0 =$ ___

p. $4 \times 3 =$ ___

q. $3 \times 3 =$ ___

r. $7 \times 3 =$ ___

s. $6 \times 4 =$ ___

t. $5 \times 2 =$ ___

u. $5 \times 4 =$ ___

v. $6 \times 3 =$ ___

w. $6 \times 5 =$ ___

x. $4 \times 6 =$ ___

y. $3 \times 6 =$ ___

z. $6 \times 6 =$ ___

Name_____

Multiply to solve the problems. Color a section of the thermometer for each row you complete.

a. 7
×0

b. 6
×1

c. 4
×1

d. 3
×2

e. 5
×0

f. 6
×0

g. 1
×6

h. 3
×5

i. 2
×7

j. 6
×2

k. 4
×4

l. 5
×7

m. 6
×4

n. 3
×3

o. 2
×4

p. 4
×5

q. 6
×3

r. 4
×6

s. 7
×2

t. 5
×6

u. 7
×1

v. 2
×6

w. 4
×3

x. 5
×4

Name _____

Divide to solve the problems. Help the mouse find the cheese.

Start →

a.	b.	c.	d.
$1\overline{)4}$	$6\overline{)6}$	$2\overline{)12}$	$3\overline{)6}$

				e.
				$7\overline{)21}$

j.	i.	h.	g.	f.
$6\overline{)24}$	$7\overline{)42}$	$4\overline{)28}$	$5\overline{)35}$	$5\overline{)20}$

k.				
$5\overline{)15}$				

l.	m.	n.	o.	p.
$2\overline{)14}$	$7\overline{)14}$	$3\overline{)21}$	$6\overline{)36}$	$3\overline{)3}$

				q.
				$1\overline{)7}$

		t.	s.	r.
		$3\overline{)18}$	$7\overline{)49}$	$6\overline{)30}$

Finish

Name_____

Multiply to solve the problems.

a.
$6 \times 2 =$ _____

b.
$7 \times 5 =$ _____

c.
$7 \times 3 =$ _____

d.
$2 \times 0 =$ _____

e.
$7 \times 6 =$ _____

f.
$3 \times 5 =$ _____

g.
$0 \times 0 =$ _____

h.
$0 \times 4 =$ _____

i.
$3 \times 4 =$ _____

j.
$2 \times 5 =$ _____

k.
$4 \times 5 =$ _____

l.
$1 \times 6 =$ _____

m.
$2 \times 7 =$ _____

n.
$3 \times 6 =$ _____

o.
$5 \times 5 =$ _____

(c) Carson-Dellosa Publ. CD-0926

Name_____

Divide to solve the problems.

a. 3)‾12‾

b. 2)‾2‾

c. 5)‾35‾

d. 1)‾4‾

e. 3)‾15‾

h. 6)‾24‾

g. 5)‾20‾

f. 6)‾36‾

i. 5)‾10‾

j. 7)‾28‾

k. 4)‾28‾

l. 4)‾12‾

m. 6)‾18‾

q. 1)‾6‾

p. 7)‾49‾

o. 2)‾8‾

n. 5)‾30‾

41

Name_____

Multiply to solve the problems and color:

0 = red   6 = blue   10 = green
4 = yellow 8 = pink   12 = orange

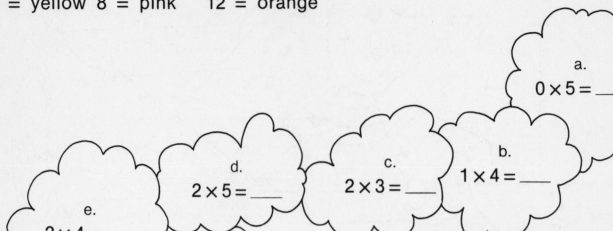

a.
0 × 5 = ___

b.
1 × 4 = ___

c.
2 × 3 = ___

d.
2 × 5 = ___

e.
2 × 4 = ___

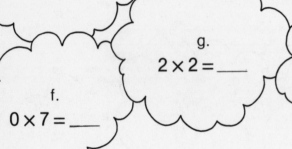

f.
0 × 7 = ___

g.
2 × 2 = ___

h.
5 × 2 = ___

i.
3 × 4 = ___

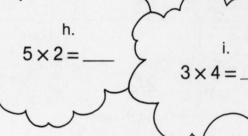

j.
6 × 1 = ___

k.
2 × 6 = ___

l.
2 × 0 = ___

m.
3 × 2 = ___

n.
3 × 0 = ___

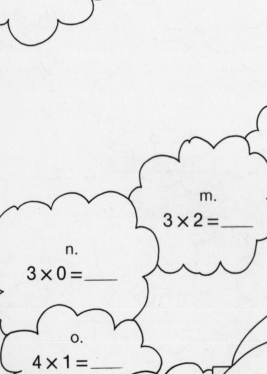

o.
4 × 1 = ___

p.
4 × 2 = ___

© Carson-Dellosa Publ. CD-0926

Name _____

Multiply to solve the problems and color:

4 = orange
6 = red
12 = yellow
24 = green
36 = blue
42 = purple

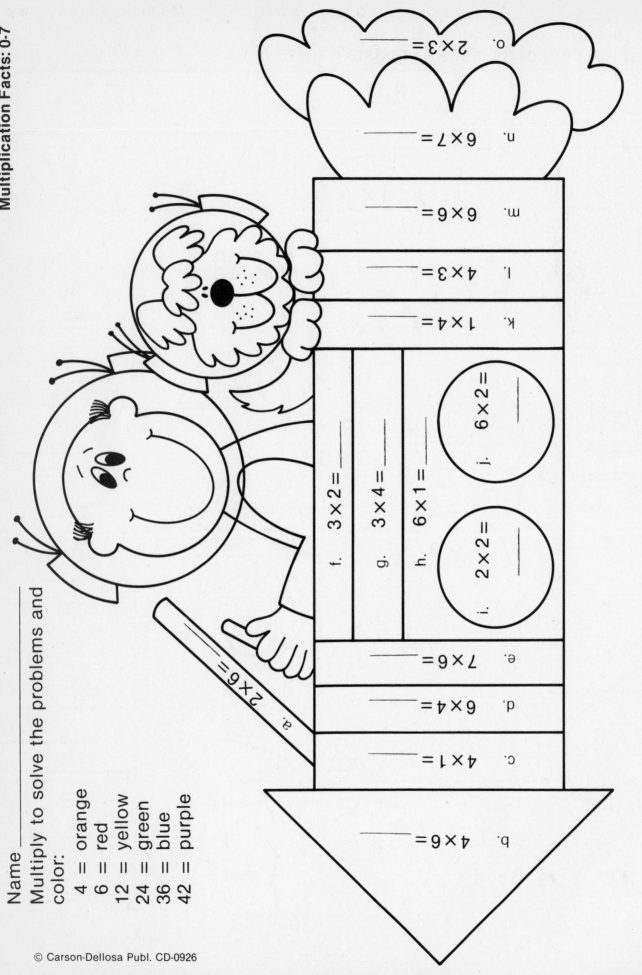

a. 2 × 6 = _____

b. 4 × 6 = _____

c. 4 × 1 = _____

d. 6 × 4 = _____

e. 7 × 6 = _____

f. 3 × 2 = _____

g. 3 × 4 = _____

h. 6 × 1 = _____

i. 2 × 2 = _____

j. 6 × 2 = _____

k. 1 × 4 = _____

l. 4 × 3 = _____

m. 6 × 6 = _____

n. 6 × 7 = _____

o. 2 × 3 = _____

Name_____

Multiply to solve the problems. Cut out each answer at the right of the page and paste it to the correct tennis ball.

a. 2×6

b. 3×7

c. 5×6

d. 4×6

e. 7×7

f. 0×6

g. 6×3

h. 5×3

i. 5×2

j. 4×1

k. 3×2

l. 7×6

m. 2×0

n. 6×6

o. 6×4

p. 5×7

0
24
21
10
42
36
6
4
15
12
30
24
18
49
35
0

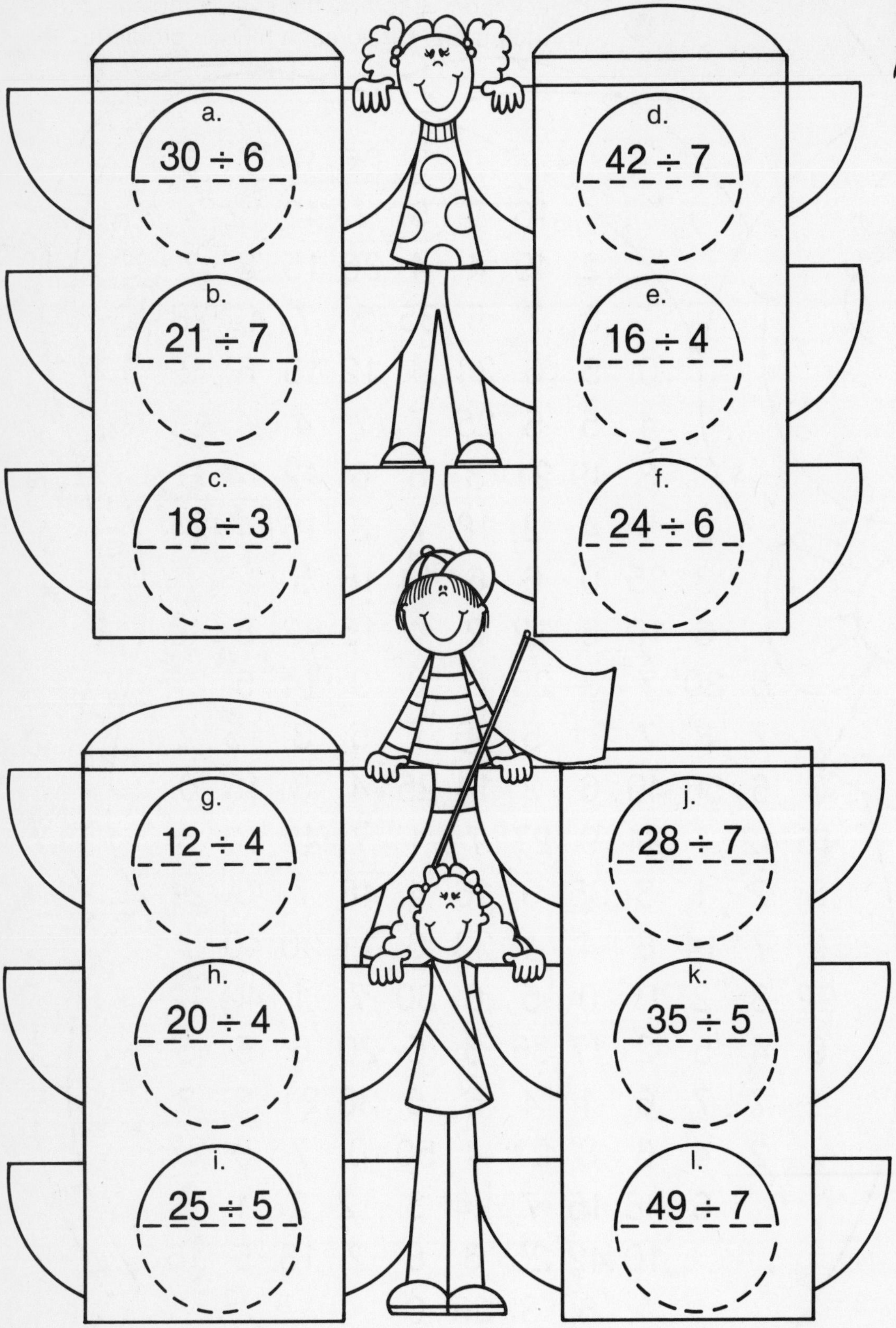
a. 30 ÷ 6
b. 21 ÷ 7
c. 18 ÷ 3
d. 42 ÷ 7
e. 16 ÷ 4
f. 24 ÷ 6
g. 12 ÷ 4
h. 20 ÷ 4
i. 25 ÷ 5
j. 28 ÷ 7
k. 35 ÷ 5
l. 49 ÷ 7

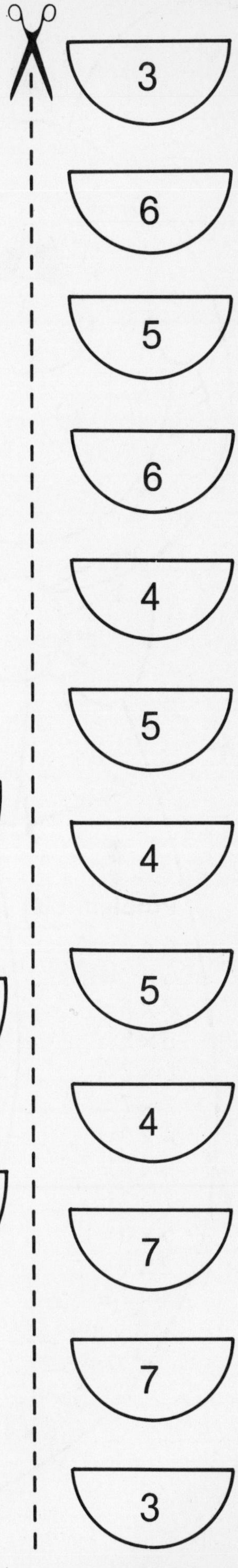
3
6
5
6
4
5
4
5
4
7
7
3

Name____

Divide to solve the problems. Cut out each answer at the right of the page and paste it to the correct traffic light.

Name _____

Multiply to solve the problems in the problem list. Use × and = to find the same problems hidden in the puzzle. Circle each hidden problem.

```
        3  25  9   7   5
   16  0 (6 X 7 = 42) 12  4   6
    2  49  4   4  36  15  8   7   5
    3   7  5  35   3   7  42  28 10
  0  5  6  24  4  12  18  6   2   3
  4  5  5  25  7   7   4   4  16  15
  8  49 21  3   6   6  42  14  0
  8  5  4   2  18  7   3  16  (4) 24
  3  35  0  6   6  14  18  5   (X2=8) 7
  6  10  8  12  2   4  15  32  (8) 49
 5  30  7   3  25  6   2   9  14  5  27
7  7  8  7  21  5  36  7   5   3  15  2
3  6 56 49  6   2  14 25   4   8  18  0
15 42 7  24  9  27  7   1   7  42 10  5
8  2  1   3  35  9  16  4  48  7   3  21
2  7  14  8   4   4  33  6  11  20 40  7
22 8  2  15   0   5   6 30   7   1  42 12
9  4  5   2  17 36   8  5  20   6   5   5
   7  7   6   1   4   6   5 36  21   3   8
   2  4   6   8  27  4  50   0   7   0  27
      6 36  15  7  24   3  12   2   1   3
     10 42  25  6   8   2  18   5  16
      6   3  25  0
```

Problem List

4 × 4 = _____
6 × 7 = _____
7 × 7 = _____
5 × 5 = _____
0 × 7 = _____
2 × 7 = _____
4 × 2 = _____
6 × 6 = _____
7 × 3 = _____
5 × 3 = _____
2 × 6 = _____
4 × 7 = _____
6 × 3 = _____
7 × 5 = _____
5 × 6 = _____
6 × 4 = _____
7 × 1 = _____
7 × 6 = _____

46

Name_____

Divide to solve the problems in the problem list. Use ÷ and = to find the same problems hidden in the puzzle. Circle each hidden problem.

Problem List

49 ÷ 7 = ___	30 ÷ 6 = ___	36 ÷ 6 = ___	25 ÷ 5 = ___	21 ÷ 3 = ___
18 ÷ 6 = ___	12 ÷ 4 = ___	16 ÷ 4 = ___	9 ÷ 3 = ___	42 ÷ 6 = ___
42 ÷ 7 = ___	0 ÷ 4 = ___	21 ÷ 7 = ___	35 ÷ 7 = ___	20 ÷ 4 = ___
	28 ÷ 4 = ___	30 ÷ 5 = ___	15 ÷ 3 = ___	

```
36   6   7  12   4   3   9   1  (16÷4=4) 15   3   4
35   4   6   0   3   5  32   3  28   8  36   6  (28   2
 7  24   4   4  49   3  36  25   5  49   7  12   4    0
 5  42   7   0   5  21   6   5  18  15   3   5   7)  49
15   3   9  10  36   9   6   5  32   4  16   8  27   7
36   9   8  27   3  12   8  24  30   6   5  40   9   8
18   2   7  18  40   5  36   7  20  30   5   4   6   2
30  21  12   6   4  20   9  30   5   6   9   3  21  20
27   3   8   3  49   7   9   3   3  28   2  15   7   4
 5   7  42   9  16   2  35   7  18   3   4  30   3   5
36   7   3  27   3   4  42   6   7  49   7   2  16   3
 4  49   7   7  16   4   1  14  42   7   6   5  32   1
```

Name_____

Multiply to solve the problems.

a.
$$\begin{array}{r} 4 \\ \times 8 \\ \hline \end{array}$$

b.
$$\begin{array}{r} 4 \\ \times 5 \\ \hline \end{array}$$

c.
$$\begin{array}{r} 5 \\ \times 9 \\ \hline \end{array}$$

d.
$$\begin{array}{r} 1 \\ \times 7 \\ \hline \end{array}$$

e.
$$\begin{array}{r} 5 \\ \times 7 \\ \hline \end{array}$$

f.
$$\begin{array}{r} 4 \\ \times 4 \\ \hline \end{array}$$

g.
$$\begin{array}{r} 7 \\ \times 8 \\ \hline \end{array}$$

h.
$$\begin{array}{r} 1 \\ \times 0 \\ \hline \end{array}$$

i.
$$\begin{array}{r} 6 \\ \times 9 \\ \hline \end{array}$$

j.
$$\begin{array}{r} 3 \\ \times 0 \\ \hline \end{array}$$

k.
$$\begin{array}{r} 4 \\ \times 1 \\ \hline \end{array}$$

l.
$$\begin{array}{r} 8 \\ \times 2 \\ \hline \end{array}$$

m.
$$\begin{array}{r} 1 \\ \times 9 \\ \hline \end{array}$$

n.
$$\begin{array}{r} 8 \\ \times 6 \\ \hline \end{array}$$

o.
$$\begin{array}{r} 5 \\ \times 6 \\ \hline \end{array}$$

p.
$$\begin{array}{r} 3 \\ \times 8 \\ \hline \end{array}$$

q.
$$\begin{array}{r} 7 \\ \times 2 \\ \hline \end{array}$$

Name_____

Multiply to solve the problems. Start at the bottom and follow the path to the mitten.

s. 7
   ×6

r. 2
   ×7

q. 4
   ×5

p. 3
   ×3

t. 3
   ×6

Finish

o. 9
   ×7

n. 7
   ×9

m. 0
   ×6

l. 8
   ×8

h. 4
   ×4

i. 3
   ×2

j. 5
   ×7

k. 2
   ×2

g. 4
   ×1

f. 8
   ×4

e. 5
   ×9

d. 8
   ×7

c. 1
   ×9

b. 9
   ×8

a. 3
   ×7

Start

a. $\begin{array}{r} 8 \\ \times 0 \\ \hline \end{array}$

b. $\begin{array}{r} 6 \\ \times 4 \\ \hline \end{array}$

c. $\begin{array}{r} 9 \\ \times 7 \\ \hline \end{array}$

d. $\begin{array}{r} 7 \\ \times 3 \\ \hline \end{array}$

e. $\begin{array}{r} 4 \\ \times 1 \\ \hline \end{array}$

g. $\begin{array}{r} 7 \\ \times 1 \\ \hline \end{array}$

h. $\begin{array}{r} 2 \\ \times 6 \\ \hline \end{array}$

i. $\begin{array}{r} 1 \\ \times 3 \\ \hline \end{array}$

j. $\begin{array}{r} 9 \\ \times 8 \\ \hline \end{array}$

f. $\begin{array}{r} 1 \\ \times 6 \\ \hline \end{array}$

Multiply or divide to solve the problems. See if you can get to the "core" of the problems.

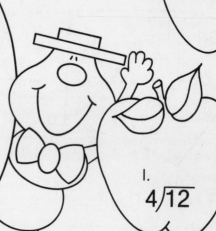

k. $3\overline{)27}$

l. $4\overline{)12}$

m. $2\overline{)16}$

n. $8\overline{)56}$

o. $5\overline{)5}$

p. $4\overline{)16}$

q. $8\overline{)8}$

r. $9\overline{)36}$

s. $4\overline{)32}$

t. $9\overline{)27}$

Name_____

Divide to solve the problems. See how many baskets you can make!

a. $2\overline{)18}$

b. $7\overline{)49}$

c. $6\overline{)54}$

d. $8\overline{)32}$

e. $9\overline{)27}$

f. $4\overline{)16}$

g. $8\overline{)72}$

h. $7\overline{)63}$

i. $5\overline{)30}$

j. $4\overline{)28}$

k. $8\overline{)64}$

l. $3\overline{)24}$

m. $9\overline{)45}$

n. $3\overline{)21}$

o. $4\overline{)36}$

p. $6\overline{)42}$

q. $4\overline{)20}$

r. $8\overline{)56}$

s. $5\overline{)25}$

t. $6\overline{)48}$

u. $2\overline{)12}$

v. $5\overline{)35}$

w. $9\overline{)81}$

x. $8\overline{)40}$

Multiplication and Division Facts: 0-9

Name_____

a. $9 \times 2 =$ _____

b. $9 \times 0 =$ _____

c. $6 \times 7 =$ _____

d. $1 \times 5 =$ _____

e. $8 \times 4 =$ _____

f. $8 \times 7 =$ _____

g. $8 \times 9 =$ _____

h. $4 \times 4 =$ _____

i. $4 \times 7 =$ _____

j. $6 \times 9 =$ _____

k. $24 \div 8 =$ _____

l. $2 \div 1 =$ _____

m. $28 \div 4 =$ _____

n. $42 \div 6 =$ _____

o. $27 \div 9 =$ _____

p. $64 \div 8 =$ _____

q. $14 \div 2 =$ _____

r. $21 \div 7 =$ _____

s. $35 \div 5 =$ _____

t. $63 \div 7 =$ _____

u. $49 \div 7 =$ _____

Multiply or divide to solve the problems and "sharpen" your math skills.

© Carson-Dellosa Publ. CD-0926

Name_____

Multiply or divide to solve the problems.

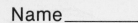
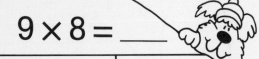

a.

$9 \times 8 = $ ___

b.

$32 \div 8 = $ ___

c.

$40 \div 8 = $ ___

d.

$7 \times 5 = $ ___

e.

$9 \times 6 = $ ___

f.

$45 \div 5 = $ ___

g.

$42 \div 7 = $ ___

h.

$6 \times 6 = $ ___

i.

$5 \times 4 = $ ___

j.

$32 \div 4 = $ ___

k.

$36 \div 6 = $ ___

l.

$12 \div 2 = $ ___

m.

$6 \times 3 = $ ___

n.

$5 \times 9 = $ ___

o.

$8 \times 0 = $ ___

p.

$25 \div 5 = $ ___

q.

$28 \div 4 = $ ___

r.

$3 \div 3 = $ ___

s.

$5 \times 0 = $ ___

t.

$4 \times 1 = $ ___

u.

$2 \times 6 = $ ___

53

Name _____

Divide to solve the problems and color:

2 = brown   5 = purple   7 = orange   9 = black
            6 = green   8 = yellow

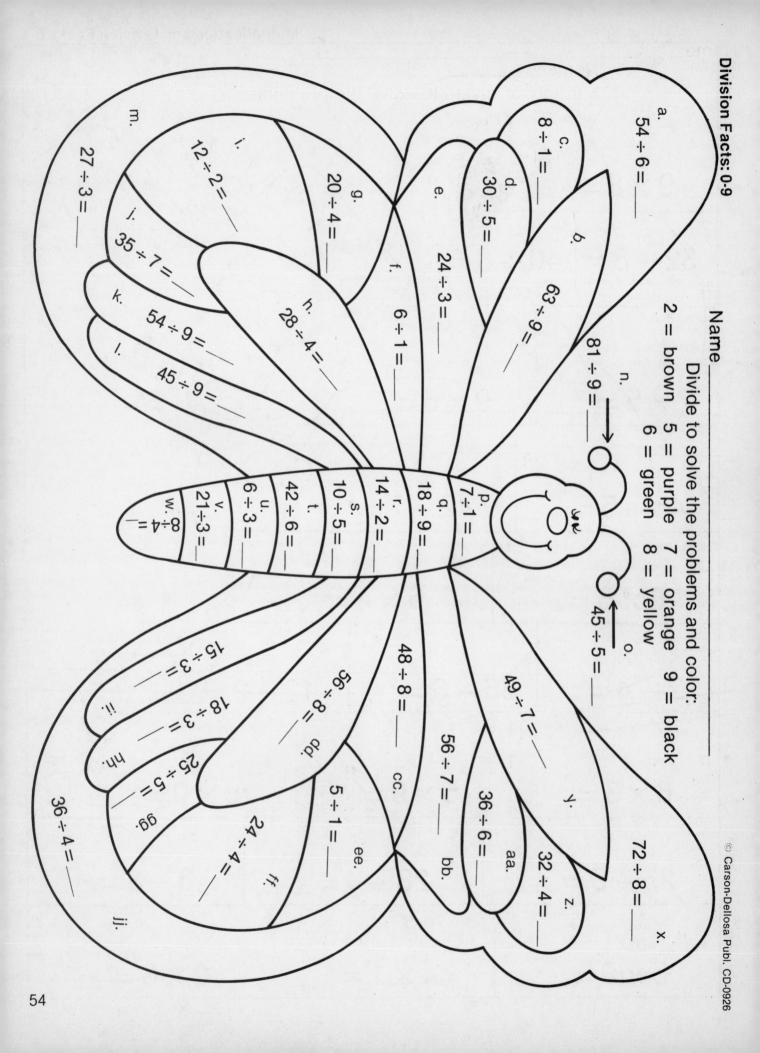

a. $54 \div 6 =$ ___

c. $8 \div 1 =$ ___

d. $30 \div 5 =$ ___

e. $24 \div 3 =$ ___

b. $63 \div 9 =$ ___

f. $6 \div 1 =$ ___

g. $20 \div 4 =$ ___

h. $28 \div 4 =$ ___

i. $12 \div 2 =$ ___

j. $35 \div 7 =$ ___

k. $54 \div 9 =$ ___

l. $45 \div 9 =$ ___

m. $27 \div 3 =$ ___

n. $81 \div 9 =$ ___

o. $45 \div 5 =$ ___

p. $7 \div 1 =$ ___

q. $18 \div 9 =$ ___

r. $14 \div 2 =$ ___

s. $10 \div 5 =$ ___

t. $42 \div 6 =$ ___

u. $6 \div 3 =$ ___

v. $21 \div 3 =$ ___

w. $8 \div 4 =$ ___

x. $72 \div 8 =$ ___

y. $32 \div 4 =$ ___

z. $32 \div 4 =$ ___

aa. $36 \div 6 =$ ___

bb. $56 \div 7 =$ ___

cc. $49 \div 7 =$ ___

dd. $56 \div 8 =$ ___

ee. $5 \div 1 =$ ___

ff. $24 \div 4 =$ ___

gg. $25 \div 5 =$ ___

hh. $18 \div 3 =$ ___

ii. $15 \div 3 =$ ___

jj. $36 \div 4 =$ ___

48 ÷ 8 = ___

© Carson-Dellosa Publ. CD-0926

Name_____

Divide to solve the problems and color:

3 = brown
4 = blue
5 = yellow
6 = orange
7 = purple
8 = red
9 = green

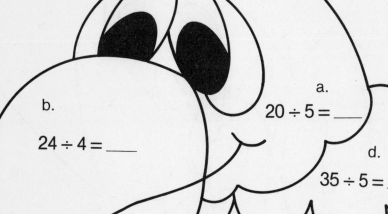

a. $20 \div 5 =$ ___

b. $24 \div 4 =$ ___

d. $35 \div 5 =$ ___

c. $12 \div 2 =$ ___

j. $81 \div 9 =$ ___

g. $10 \div 2 =$ ___

h. $18 \div 3 =$ ___

e. $36 \div 4 =$ ___

f. $27 \div 3 =$ ___

i. $30 \div 6 =$ ___

k. $18 \div 2 =$ ___

l. $27 \div 9 =$ ___

m. $21 \div 7 =$ ___

r. $24 \div 3 =$ ___

q. $49 \div 7 =$ ___

n. $16 \div 2 =$ ___

o. $32 \div 8 =$ ___

p. $45 \div 5 =$ ___

55

Name_____

Multiply or divide to solve the problems and color:

7 = orange   9 = black   18 = purple   32 = red
8 = yellow   16 = blue   24 = green   36 = brown

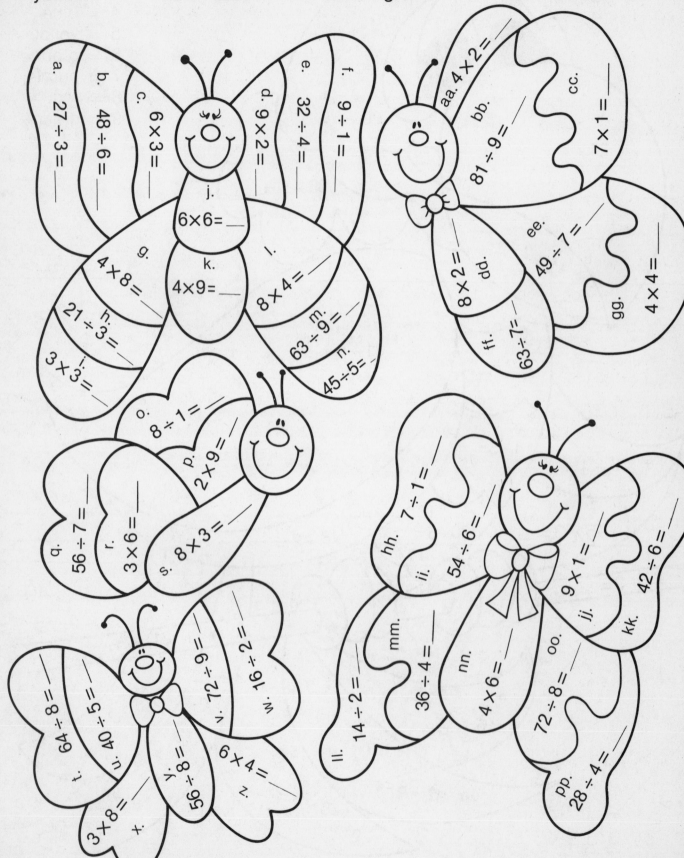

a. 27 ÷ 3 =
b. 48 ÷ 6 =
c. 6 × 3 =
d. 9 × 2 =
e. 32 ÷ 4 =
f. 9 ÷ 1 =
g. 4 × 8 =
h. 21 ÷ 3 =
i. 3 × 3 =
j. 6 × 6 =
k. 4 × 9 =
l. 8 × 4 =
m. 63 ÷ 9 =
n. 45 ÷ 5 =
o. 8 ÷ 1 =
p. 2 × 9 =
q. 56 ÷ 7 =
r. 3 × 6 =
s. 8 × 3 =

aa. 4 × 2 =
bb. 81 ÷ 9 =
cc. 7 × 1 =
dd. 8 × 2 =
ee. 49 ÷ 7 =
ff. 63 ÷ 7 =
gg. 4 × 4 =

t. 64 ÷ 8 =
u. 40 ÷ 5 =
v. 72 ÷ 9 =
w. 16 ÷ 2 =
x. 3 × 8 =
y. 56 ÷ 8 =
z. 6 × 4 =

hh. 7 ÷ 1 =
ii. 54 ÷ 6 =
jj. 9 × 1 =
kk. 42 ÷ 6 =
ll. 14 ÷ 2 =
mm. 36 ÷ 4 =
nn. 4 × 6 =
oo. 72 ÷ 8 =
pp. 28 ÷ 4 =

Name_____

Multiply to solve the problems at the bottom of the page. Cut out each problem and paste it to the heart with the correct answer.

a. 32

b. 40

c. 42

d. 27

e. 48

f. 36

g. 28

h. 81

i. 45

j. 54

k. 24

l. 30

m. 64

n. 49

5 × 9

7 × 7

9 × 9

5 × 6

6 × 7

4 × 9

4 × 8

4 × 6

6 × 9

8 × 8

7 × 4

8 × 6

5 × 8

3 × 9

4	
5	
3	
6	
9	
8	
6	
9	
9	
7	
4	
9	

Name_____

Divide to solve the problems. Cut out each answer at the left of the page and paste it to the correct box.

a.
81 ÷ 9

b.
64 ÷ 8

c.
54 ÷ 9

d.
49 ÷ 7

e.
42 ÷ 7

f.
45 ÷ 5

g.
36 ÷ 9

h.
32 ÷ 8

i.
27 ÷ 3

j.
25 ÷ 5

k.
18 ÷ 2

l.
12 ÷ 4

58

© Carson-Dellosa Publ. CD-0926

```
            0   9        1   4
        2   8   4  37  8   0   5   8  45
    0   8   6   6  39  4   3   6  18   8
  8  5   7   4  28  8   8  54  8   8  26  2   3
  3  6  16  9   3   9  9  81 18  9   3  18  4   9
  7  5  33  5   8  40  0   7   9   3  27  7   0   6
  4  9  38  9  27  8   8  64  4  28  49 35  28  9
  1  0 (7×7=49) 9   8   4  35  0   9   6   6  36  6  24
  6  4   9  36  6  37  6   7  12  7   7  45  7   4  32  9
  3  2  28 10   5   8  35  5   5   4  63  7   4  30  8   6
  8  3   8  21  8   4  42 35  9   0   3   6   8   3   0   1
  = 7  7  48  9  36  18 32   5   8   5  40   0   8   1  15
 24 64  3   7   4   9   4  36  63  7   5  33 12   2   9   7  66
  4   0   8   0  32   5   8  48  9   7   9   2  18  9   3  21
  8   8  76   4   9   8   4  32   2  32   8   3   0  80   8  56
     3  21   9  72  39   2   5  24   6        9   1   9
        9  33  28                           3   6  28
               4                         0  37   9   5
```

(with circled: 7×7=49, and vertically 3×8=24)

Problem List

9 × 1 = _____   9 × 9 = _____
8 × 5 = _____   3 × 8 = _____
7 × 5 = _____   4 × 9 = _____
9 × 3 = _____   3 × 6 = _____
7 × 7 = _____   0 × 8 = _____
6 × 6 = _____   9 × 4 = _____
7 × 4 = _____
8 × 4 = _____
9 × 2 = _____
8 × 8 = _____
9 × 7 = _____
5 × 8 = _____

Multiply to solve the problems in the problem list. Use × and = to find the same problems hidden in the puzzle. Circle each hidden problem.

Name_____

Divide to solve the problems in the problem list. Use ÷ and = to find the same problems in the puzzle. Circle each hidden problem.

```
40  72  24   6              48   8    7
 5  (36 ÷ 4 = 9)   8    2   27   3    9   32  48
 9   1   9   54  81   27   3    7    9    1   32
45   9   6    2   45    9  18    2   24    6    4    8
56   8   6   72    9    9   2   54    6    4   81    4
 8  42   7    9    5   27   9    4   64    6   (18)   8
 7  40  63    8   30    5   7   49    8   56   (3)  21
48  63   7    9   42    7   6   48    8    8   (6)  63
32   8   2   72    6   20  42    7   16    4    4   72    7
 8  54   6    9    1    4  36   64    8    4   48    8    6
 3  45   9    9    0   24  40    5    8   63   32    8    3
```

Problem List

81 ÷ 9 = _____	18 ÷ 2 = _____	16 ÷ 4 = _____	56 ÷ 8 = _____
9 ÷ 1 = _____	24 ÷ 6 = _____	40 ÷ 5 = _____	45 ÷ 9 = _____
27 ÷ 3 = _____	32 ÷ 8 = _____	48 ÷ 8 = _____	72 ÷ 9 = _____
36 ÷ 4 = _____	18 ÷ 3 = _____	42 ÷ 7 = _____	54 ÷ 6 = _____
		63 ÷ 7 = _____	64 ÷ 8 = _____

© Carson-Dellosa Publ. CD-0926

Answer Key

Test 1 ×

A 12, 3, 4, 25, 15, 0, 8, 4, 0, 10
B 25, 8, 0, 16, 5, 6, 20, 10, 0, 9
C 0, 3, 5, 20, 0, 1, 4, 0, 0, 2
D 6, 12, 0, 15, 10, 16, 0, 3, 10, 2
E 0, 3, 2, 6, 0, 4, 12, 0, 15, 5
F 8, 0, 0, 8, 9, 5, 1, 4, 0, 0
G 20, 2, 0, 5, 0, 16, 2, 10, 5, 8
H 0, 10, 4, 0, 6, 3, 15, 0, 4, 12
I 20, 0, 6, 12, 1, 6, 15, 2, 4, 25
J 12, 0, 20, 4, 15, 0, 20, 3, 8, 9

Test 2 ×

A 3, 10, 4, 12, 20, 0, 9, 0, 6, 12
B 0, 25, 4, 8, 1, 10, 16, 2, 0, 15
C 5, 0, 12, 6, 5, 0, 6, 10, 3, 2
D 0, 9, 5, 0, 3, 20, 8, 0, 1, 25
E 16, 4, 0, 4, 12, 0, 15, 2, 0, 15
F 5, 9, 0, 10, 4, 4, 20, 0, 0, 15
G 8, 2, 4, 1, 10, 6, 3, 12, 6, 0
H 2, 0, 5, 3, 15, 0, 20, 0, 25, 0
I 0, 8, 15, 4, 8, 0, 12, 20, 0, 4
J 8, 0, 0, 6, 5, 3, 20, 10, 2, 16

Test 3 ×

A 12, 0, 35, 30, 9, 21, 5, 16, 24, 20
B 0, 49, 6, 1, 18, 10, 30, 4, 0, 35
C 30, 18, 12, 7, 0, 28, 15, 4, 42, 15
D 35, 4, 0, 6, 12, 0, 6, 20, 14, 12
E 2, 15, 28, 0, 8, 36, 20, 6, 10, 0
F 14, 15, 8, 25, 6, 12, 10, 0, 21, 24
G 20, 8, 0, 42, 18, 12, 14, 49, 3, 4
H 2, 21, 36, 16, 10, 0, 35, 24, 3, 42
I 0, 12, 7, 28, 18, 5, 0, 24, 8, 9
J 0, 6, 42, 12, 0, 28, 25, 21, 30, 14

Test 4 ×

A 36, 3, 0, 8, 0, 16, 30, 6, 18, 20
B 30, 5, 7, 21, 28, 6, 24, 0, 6, 12
C 20, 9, 49, 8, 30, 0, 14, 18, 28, 42
D 25, 0, 3, 42, 15, 24, 35, 2, 0, 35
E 21, 0, 12, 20, 3, 0, 28, 10, 7, 12
F 5, 15, 0, 21, 12, 35, 4, 12, 0, 8
G 49, 10, 24, 0, 20, 2, 12, 42, 4, 6
H 16, 12, 6, 0, 1, 42, 10, 0, 18, 21
I 2, 9, 6, 4, 36, 7, 0, 28, 14, 30
J 35, 0, 5, 15, 14, 4, 18, 24, 25, 15

Test 5 ×

A 0, 10, 0, 18, 20, 14, 42, 18, 42, 1
B 40, 6, 24, 8, 63, 0, 3, 21, 6, 32
C 35, 9, 4, 6, 0, 15, 81, 12, 45, 0
D 16, 36, 28, 0, 63, 9, 25, 2, 0, 8
E 0, 64, 15, 24, 4, 5, 7, 32, 0, 27
F 7, 12, 40, 3, 0, 6, 35, 0, 18, 8
G 18, 0, 0, 20, 16, 56, 0, 54, 0, 36
H 72, 2, 45, 28, 0, 4, 21, 72, 9, 56
I 24, 54, 8, 30, 12, 0, 10, 16, 0, 49
J 5, 27, 12, 0, 48, 30, 36, 24, 14, 48

Test 6 ×

A 16, 32, 3, 42, 0, 27, 8, 30, 0, 35
B 14, 18, 0, 54, 0, 21, 45, 24, 40, 5
C 4, 64, 0, 24, 10, 36, 0, 56, 16, 9
D 15, 48, 6, 32, 12, 8, 28, 0, 18, 9
E 12, 6, 0, 35, 0, 72, 36, 7, 0, 20
F 0, 72, 3, 49, 10, 6, 0, 2, 56, 25
G 30, 27, 0, 63, 8, 5, 1, 8, 4, 63
H 40, 4, 21, 15, 45, 14, 36, 12, 24, 0
I 2, 48, 0, 9, 81, 16, 0, 42, 6, 20
J 28, 0, 54, 24, 0, 12, 0, 18, 7, 18

Test 7 ×

A 63, 32, 27, 30, 0, 12, 6, 16, 6, 0
B 12, 25, 0, 56, 9, 0, 81, 0, 54, 42
C 63, 12, 21, 0, 35, 0, 3, 45, 20, 14
D 7, 27, 6, 0, 40, 0, 4, 36, 0, 48
E 28, 24, 18, 6, 10, 2, 48, 9, 0, 18
F 15, 20, 0, 56, 8, 16, 7, 12, 0, 8
G 40, 3, 24, 0, 35, 72, 5, 16, 36, 10
H 0, 54, 0, 21, 2, 64, 24, 8, 0, 36
I 49, 45, 0, 14, 1, 4, 42, 15, 72, 9
J 8, 30, 4, 24, 32, 18, 5, 0, 28, 18

Test 8 ×

A 24, 54, 24, 0, 2, 9, 0, 27, 20, 8
B 6, 42, 0, 5, 8, 24, 21, 0, 24, 45
C 48, 16, 0, 3, 12, 35, 2, 48, 15, 72
D 63, 1, 0, 14, 20, 6, 0, 45, 0, 16
E 12, 7, 72, 42, 0, 14, 35, 21, 6, 4
F 12, 10, 8, 40, 18, 30, 36, 0, 81, 5
G 64, 0, 9, 27, 6, 32, 0, 15, 56, 36
H 0, 18, 4, 7, 0, 63, 16, 9, 3, 56
I 12, 28, 25, 0, 32, 40, 0, 8, 0, 18
J 30, 4, 10, 36, 49, 18, 0, 54, 0, 28

Answer Key

Test 9 ×

A 18, 14, 3, 42, 0, 20, 9, 12, 63, 20
B 8, 5, 0, 4, 0, 32, 6, 56, 0, 45
C 5, 27, 8, 0, 30, 0, 56, 16, 15, 0
D 42, 10, 18, 16, 32, 2, 40, 0, 28, 24
E 36, 0, 21, 48, 6, 7, 15, 54, 8, 24
F 6, 64, 28, 3, 10, 0, 12, 4, 0, 14
G 25, 0, 24, 2, 54, 0, 12, 35, 9, 72
H 72, 4, 0, 7, 24, 0, 27, 45, 8, 49
I 0, 48, 0, 21, 1, 40, 0, 63, 6, 16
J 18, 30, 18, 36, 0, 81, 36, 12, 35, 9

Test 10 ×

A 28, 24, 3, 45, 4, 32, 6, 48, 0, 25
B 8, 0, 0, 12, 15, 18, 21, 0, 72, 14
C 20, 0, 56, 0, 5, 28, 6, 9, 24, 0
D 7, 36, 8, 42, 0, 0, 45, 42, 3, 12
E 0, 40, 6, 30, 1, 36, 0, 4, 12, 20
F 49, 27, 5, 0, 36, 4, 12, 24, 0, 10
G 27, 9, 0, 16, 0, 40, 81, 2, 64, 0
H 16, 6, 54, 7, 35, 32, 0, 72, 21, 63
I 35, 0, 24, 9, 15, 18, 48, 14, 2, 63
J 16, 18, 0, 56, 10, 18, 8, 54, 8, 30

Test 11 ×

A 9, 40, 10, 35, 28
B 0, 0, 48, 0, 18
C 54, 28, 0, 16, 0
D 24, 7, 21, 3, 15
E 81, 27, 0, 63, 0
F 3, 32, 35, 10, 2
G 36, 0, 7, 0, 18
H 12, 56, 8, 40, 2
I 24, 72, 5, 0, 21
J 8, 30, 0, 12, 0

K 63, 0, 36, 6, 18
L 0, 54, 6, 72, 0
M 14, 12, 0, 15, 24
N 6, 45, 8, 1, 49
O 30, 0, 25, 18, 16
P 27, 6, 5, 16, 4
Q 4, 9, 36, 0, 42
R 32, 20, 42, 45, 20
S 64, 48, 0, 9, 56
T 12, 4, 14, 24, 8

Test 12 ×

A 42, 24, 10, 0, 35
B 5, 72, 16, 7, 8
C 42, 0, 6, 36, 18
D 30, 18, 0, 24, 0
E 54, 8, 81, 0, 9
F 2, 35, 18, 3, 20
G 0, 21, 0, 63, 9
H 12, 32, 36, 6, 25
I 16, 0, 40, 4, 28
J 0, 1, 6, 54, 12

K 48, 8, 5, 0, 4
L 15, 4, 0, 16, 64
M 0, 32, 30, 14, 18
N 45, 3, 0, 56, 8
O 27, 14, 0, 2, 0
P 72, 0, 9, 45, 21
Q 24, 63, 7, 27, 20
R 49, 0, 40, 0, 48
S 36, 12, 56, 0, 15
T 6, 10, 12, 28, 24

Test 1 ÷

A 1, 2, 5, 0, 3, 3, 2, 2, 4, 5
B 5, 4, 2, 1, 5, 2, 1, 5, 5, 4
C 2, 3, 1, 1, 0, 1, 5, 4, 4, 0
D 5, 5, 4, 0, 1, 1, 4, 5, 3, 0
E 4, 0, 2, 3, 2, 4, 3, 5, 4, 3
F 0, 3, 3, 4, 5, 2, 5, 1, 5, 4
G 1, 4, 5, 1, 0, 2, 3, 3, 0, 3
H 4, 0, 5, 1, 5, 4, 2, 3, 2, 4
I 4, 1, 3, 2, 1, 2, 0, 1, 3, 5
J 1, 1, 3, 3, 2, 4, 2, 0, 2, 0

Test 2 ÷

A 1, 4, 3, 0, 2, 2, 1, 3, 3, 3
B 2, 2, 1, 3, 1, 3, 5, 3, 3, 4
C 2, 5, 3, 1, 4, 5, 3, 5, 3, 0
D 4, 4, 3, 3, 1, 3, 0, 5, 1, 4
E 5, 4, 0, 1, 2, 5, 1, 1, 3, 5
F 2, 5, 2, 4, 2, 0, 3, 3, 0, 4
G 2, 0, 4, 5, 0, 4, 2, 1, 4, 1
H 2, 2, 2, 4, 1, 4, 5, 5, 4, 1
I 5, 1, 4, 2, 2, 1, 0, 5, 5, 5
J 1, 0, 5, 1, 3, 2, 4, 5, 2, 4

Test 3 ÷

A 4, 1, 7, 6, 2, 2, 4, 3, 2, 1
B 7, 4, 1, 5, 0, 4, 6, 4, 7, 6
C 3, 4, 3, 6, 7, 7, 1, 0, 2, 1
D 2, 0, 3, 2, 5, 4, 1, 5, 2, 4
E 6, 3, 4, 1, 3, 3, 5, 6, 4, 0
F 7, 3, 2, 6, 3, 7, 0, 7, 6, 1
G 0, 6, 2, 5, 7, 3, 5, 1, 5, 6
H 6, 5, 5, 5, 1, 7, 1, 2, 1, 5
I 7, 3, 5, 1, 0, 7, 2, 4, 7, 6
J 5, 5, 6, 2, 2, 4, 4, 3, 3, 6

Test 4 ÷

A 2, 7, 6, 3, 5, 4, 7, 4, 3, 2
B 3, 4, 1, 6, 6, 1, 2, 5, 5, 4
C 6, 1, 3, 0, 7, 6, 2, 1, 2, 5
D 4, 6, 2, 4, 6, 1, 3, 4, 4, 7
E 5, 6, 0, 6, 3, 3, 2, 1, 6, 7
F 1, 2, 3, 5, 5, 5, 1, 0, 3, 7
G 7, 6, 2, 0, 5, 7, 3, 3, 5, 7
H 4, 1, 4, 1, 2, 0, 3, 2, 1, 5
I 7, 1, 2, 5, 5, 4, 0, 5, 7, 7
J 7, 4, 2, 3, 1, 4, 6, 6, 0, 6

© Carson-Dellosa Publ. CD-0926

Answer Key

Test 5 ÷

A 9, 3, 2, 4, 7, 2, 2, 3, 6, 5
B 3, 5, 0, 8, 6, 6, 6, 4, 8, 2
C 8, 7, 2, 1, 0, 9, 7, 1, 9, 3
D 3, 4, 0, 8, 4, 5, 6, 1, 0, 9
E 5, 5, 0, 9, 5, 6, 1, 4, 3, 7
F 9, 0, 2, 2, 9, 6, 1, 6, 9, 4
G 4, 8, 1, 5, 4, 0, 3, 2, 7, 7
H 3, 2, 6, 1, 1, 4, 8, 3, 6, 9
I 7, 5, 5, 8, 0, 8, 3, 9, 2, 4
J 1, 8, 7, 5, 5, 0, 8, 7, 3, 4

Test 6 ÷

A 7, 4, 1, 2, 7, 4, 3, 4, 8, 8
B 8, 9, 2, 0, 6, 8, 6, 6, 3, 5
C 6, 4, 8, 1, 2, 8, 0, 1, 5, 4
D 3, 8, 1, 3, 7, 4, 2, 6, 1, 0
E 9, 5, 3, 3, 8, 0, 4, 2, 4, 6
F 7, 4, 0, 1, 7, 3, 8, 5, 2, 7
G 9, 0, 4, 1, 9, 5, 1, 7, 8, 2
H 5, 4, 4, 0, 5, 3, 6, 1, 3, 5
I 2, 7, 3, 9, 2, 7, 9, 6, 0, 9
J 6, 5, 8, 8, 9, 8, 7, 0, 9, 2

Test 7 ÷

A 3, 6, 4, 6, 8, 6, 1, 7, 6, 4
B 2, 6, 2, 7, 3, 5, 0, 9, 1, 2
C 0, 2, 8, 8, 3, 9, 1, 6, 4, 9
D 4, 4, 9, 1, 0, 7, 1, 3, 3, 0
E 7, 2, 6, 5, 5, 6, 5, 5, 2, 1
F 8, 4, 1, 5, 6, 8, 0, 5, 4, 6
G 2, 8, 0, 3, 1, 0, 3, 9, 7, 3
H 2, 2, 8, 9, 1, 8, 4, 7, 9, 5
I 3, 5, 4, 2, 4, 9, 7, 0, 2, 5
J 9, 7, 7, 3, 0, 7, 9, 8, 8, 6

Test 8 ÷

A 2, 7, 2, 7, 5, 4, 0, 5, 9, 3
B 6, 2, 3, 3, 8, 0, 8, 9, 7, 5
C 7, 7, 8, 1, 4, 3, 1, 8, 5, 5
D 3, 0, 5, 3, 1, 8, 0, 6, 4, 3
E 7, 2, 1, 6, 1, 5, 4, 1, 8, 9
F 3, 4, 3, 0, 1, 9, 0, 4, 7, 7
G 7, 5, 8, 6, 9, 0, 1, 8, 4, 0
H 8, 9, 9, 7, 3, 3, 7, 4, 2, 2
I 2, 6, 4, 1, 2, 0, 6, 7, 9, 4
J 6, 9, 6, 6, 9, 2, 5, 6, 2, 5

Test 9 ÷

A 4, 2, 2, 8, 1, 5, 5, 8, 7, 5
B 9, 3, 3, 0, 9, 6, 1, 5, 7, 6
C 0, 4, 2, 9, 3, 8, 8, 6, 2, 3
D 3, 2, 5, 6, 0, 7, 1, 5, 6, 1
E 3, 4, 6, 7, 8, 9, 0, 4, 1, 3
F 7, 8, 7, 8, 6, 1, 8, 2, 5, 5
G 0, 3, 2, 1, 0, 9, 9, 5, 0, 4
H 3, 9, 4, 2, 8, 7, 8, 2, 7, 4
I 3, 4, 0, 8, 6, 3, 5, 5, 1, 6
J 7, 9, 3, 4, 9, 1, 0, 4, 8, 7

Test 10 ÷

A 5, 9, 6, 6, 1, 3, 2, 5, 6, 9
B 7, 8, 4, 5, 2, 5, 8, 1, 3, 3
C 7, 1, 2, 9, 3, 0, 5, 3, 0, 7
D 0, 8, 8, 0, 1, 9, 8, 2, 7, 4
E 2, 6, 9, 9, 4, 9, 1, 8, 4, 0
F 6, 0, 5, 2, 6, 0, 1, 7, 6, 4
G 3, 4, 6, 0, 2, 9, 2, 2, 1, 8
H 6, 5, 7, 8, 8, 0, 8, 3, 7, 4
I 6, 3, 7, 8, 4, 5, 1, 4, 7, 6
J 7, 3, 4, 8, 9, 3, 5, 1, 5, 4

Test 11 ÷

A 6, 8, 5, 2, 7   K 1, 9, 1, 2, 0
B 3, 3, 4, 7, 4   L 4, 9, 0, 7, 4
C 5, 6, 3, 7, 4   M 5, 4, 9, 0, 2
D 7, 3, 3, 5, 3   N 5, 8, 0, 7, 6
E 5, 8, 9, 0, 5   O 5, 6, 2, 0, 2
F 1, 3, 2, 7, 8   P 1, 0, 4, 8, 8
G 5, 7, 8, 1, 5   Q 9, 3, 6, 5, 7
H 3, 3, 9, 9, 2   R 8, 4, 1, 0, 2
I 6, 1, 3, 2, 0   S 9, 9, 6, 8, 3
J 1, 7, 4, 6, 4   T 9, 6, 1, 8, 2

Test 12 ÷

A 4, 8, 2, 6, 7   K 5, 4, 8, 7, 0
B 8, 3, 3, 8, 8   L 1, 7, 0, 1, 7
C 3, 9, 6, 1, 7   M 5, 5, 1, 4, 3
D 5, 4, 4, 6, 9   N 0, 6, 6, 3, 6
E 8, 6, 9, 1, 3   O 4, 1, 9, 0, 9
F 7, 6, 2, 2, 4   P 5, 3, 2, 1, 7
G 9, 2, 8, 3, 3   Q 1, 7, 9, 0, 7
H 8, 4, 2, 0, 8   R 8, 5, 0, 9, 6
I 3, 8, 0, 7, 5   S 5, 9, 7, 6, 4
J 0, 1, 2, 2, 7   T 5, 2, 4, 3, 5

Answer Key

Test 1 × ÷

A 0, 4, 12, 5, 21, 7, 35, 1, 7, 4
B 7, 16, 6, 3, 0, 64, 2, 8, 9, 4
C 8, 18, 45, 0, 6, 2, 0, 6, 15, 63
D 7, 4, 0, 0, 15, 4, 0, 30, 27, 1
E 1, 18, 63, 3, 5, 0, 49, 0, 2, 40
F 0, 1, 3, 0, 1, 7, 2, 20, 3, 9
G 9, 36, 0, 8, 2, 16, 9, 6, 16, 0
H 8, 10, 4, 9, 0, 6, 0, 4, 5, 54
I 35, 6, 2, 54, 8, 8, 3, 0, 0, 7
J 9, 8, 0, 1, 72, 56, 9, 0, 20, 8

Test 2 × ÷

A 8, 0, 5, 7, 5, 0, 9, 2, 15, 56
B 0, 21, 36, 0, 0, 36, 0, 24, 1, 3
C 9, 0, 3, 2, 18, 4, 6, 10, 6, 28
D 40, 7, 0, 5, 28, 4, 3, 27, 6, 2
E 9, 2, 9, 63, 0, 1, 3, 0, 8, 24
F 45, 7, 16, 0, 8, 24, 6, 18, 4, 42
G 4, 3, 3, 40, 1, 0, 6, 5, 16, 4
H 0, 7, 8, 2, 1, 0, 4, 25, 54, 7
I 0, 0, 6, 8, 0, 3, 81, 0, 8, 9
J 9, 0, 14, 30, 8, 48, 4, 7, 14, 9

Page 35:

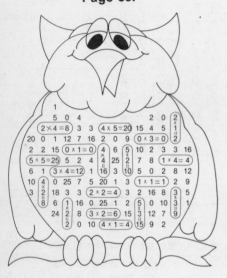

Page 36:

Page 46:

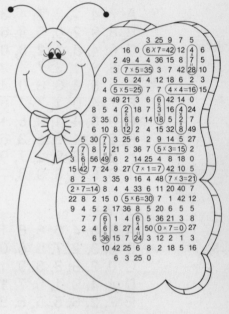

Page 47:

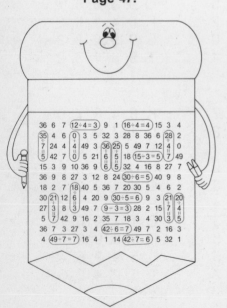

Page 59:

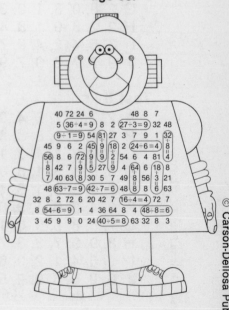

Page 60: